ARCTIC OCEAN

BEAUFORT SEA

Barrow

Point Hope

Colville River

KOTZEBUE SOUND

Noatak River

Kobuk River

Shungnak

Kotzebue

Wales

BERING STRAIT

[US-RUSSIA CONVENTION OF 1867]

USSR

USA

Gambell

ST LAWRENCE ISLAND

NOME

NORTON SOUND

Koyukuk

River

Nulato

Ruby

Tanana

YUKON

Livengood

FAIRBANKS

Fort Yukon

Porcupine River

Circle

Eagle

RIVER

UNITED STATES

CANADA

Tanana River

Big Delta

River

Jack Wade

Tok Junction

Slana

Nabesna

YUKON

ALASKA

McGrath

River

Kuskokwim

Copper Center

Chitina

Copper River

Valdez

Cordova

Willow

Palmer

Susitna River

ANCHORAGE

Whittier

Seward

Homer

Bethel

Dillingham

MONTAGUE ISLAND

Yakutat

Skagway

JUNEAU

GULF OF ALASKA

ADMIRALTY I

CHICHAGOF ISLAND

Sitka

Petersburg

BARANOF ISLAND

KUPREANOF I

Wrangell

PRINCE OF WALES ISLAND

UNITED STATES

CANADA

Ketchikan

ST MATTHEW ISLAND

BERING SEA

NUNIVAK ISLAND

PRIBILOF ISLANDS

Kodiak

KODIAK I

BRISTOL BAY

Fort Randall

PACIFIC OCEAN

ALEUTIAN ISLANDS

ALEUTIAN ISLANDS

Adak

Atka

The New
Enchantment of America
ALASKA

By Allan Carpenter

℗ CHILDRENS PRESS, CHICAGO

ACKNOWLEDGMENTS

For assistance in the preparation of the revised edition, the author thanks:
RICHARD W. MONTAGUE, Director, and NANCY ANN HARLES, Illustrations Editor, Alaska Department of Commerce and Development.

American Airlines— Anne Vitaliano, Director of Public Relations; *Capitol Historical Society,* Washington, D.C.; *Newberry Library,* Chicago, Dr. Lawrence Towner, Director; *Northwestern University Library,* Evanston, Illinois; *United Airlines*—John P. Grember, Manager of Special Promotions; Joseph P. Hopkins, Manager, News Bureau.

UNITED STATES GOVERNMENT AGENCIES: *Department of Agriculture*—Robert Hailstock, Jr., Photography Division, Office of Communication; Donald C. Schuhart, Information Division, Soil Conservation Service. *Army*—Doran Topolosky, Public Affairs Office, Chief of Engineers, Corps of Engineers. *Department of Interior*—Louis Churchville, Director of Communications; EROS Space Program—Phillis Wiepking, Community Affairs; Charles Withington, Geologist; Mrs. Ruth Herbert, Information Specialist; Bureau of Reclamation; National Park Service—Fred Bell and the individual sites; Fish and Wildlife Service— Bob Hines, Public Affairs Office. *Library of Congress*—Dr. Alan Fern, Director of the Department of Research; Sara Wallace, Director of Publications; Dr. Walter W. Ristow, Chief, Geography and Map Division; Herbert Sandborn, Exhibits Officer. *National Archives*—Dr. James B. Rhoads, Archivist of the United States; Albert Meisel, Assistant Archivist for Educational Programs; David Eggenberger, Publications Director; Bill Leary, Still Picture Reference; James Moore, Audio-Visual Archives. *United States Postal Service*—Herb Harris, Stamps Division.

For assistance in the preparation of the first edition, the author thanks:
E.L. Keithahn, Curator, Alaska State Museum and Helen Dirtadian, Director, Libraries and Museums, Department of Education, State of Alaska.

Illustrations on the preceding pages:
Cover photograph: Mountain climber near Mendenhall Glacier, State of Alaska Department of Commerce and Economic Development, Division of Tourism
Page 1: Commemorative stamps of historic interest
Pages 2-3: Scenic Glacier Bay, State of Alaska Department of Commerce and Economic Development, Division of Tourism
Page 3 (Map): USDI Geological Survey
Pages 4-5: Anchorage area, EROS Space Photo, USDI Geological Survey, EROS Data Center

Project Editor, Revised Edition:
  Joan Downing
Assistant Editor, Revised Edition:
  Mary Reidy

Library of Congress Cataloging in Publication Data

Carpenter, John Allan, 1917-
  Alaska.

  (His The new enchantment of America)
  SUMMARY: Discusses the history and geography of the state and describes its native people, minerals, and plant and animal life.
  1. Alaska—Juvenile literature.
[1. Alaska] I. Title. II. Series: Carpenter, John Allan, 1917-   The new enchantment of America.
F904.3.C3   1978   979.8   78-12419
ISBN 0-516-04102-9

Contents

A True Story to Set the Scene

A POLE STAR POINTS THE WAY

In 1926, when Alaska's American Legion decided that the territory should have a flag, they had a contest in the schools to design this important emblem.

There were many entries, but one design was so simple, professional, and significant that it was chosen the winner. The winning design was the creation of thirteen-year-old Benny Benson, an orphan from the Jesse Lee Mission Home at Seward.

In 1929, recognizing Benny's contribution, the Alaska territorial legislature awarded him $1,000 to assist with his future education. In 1963, as additional payment for his flag design, he was awarded another $2,500.

On a midnight-blue background, in Benny's design, were the seven stars of the constellation Ursa Major, the Great Bear, usually called the Big Dipper. Navigators have known for centuries that the two end stars forming the cup of the dipper point to the North Star. This they did in Benny's design, which had the pole star toward the upper-right-hand corner and of larger size than the others.

With a maturity far beyond his years, Benny had written the following description of his creation: "The blue field is for the Alaska sky and the forget-me-not, an Alaska flower. The North Star is for the future state of Alaska, the most northerly of the Union. The Dipper is for the Great Bear—symbolizing strength."

On January 3, 1959, the pole star from Benny's flag was transferred to the flag of the United States, just as he had forecast so many years before.

Benny's flag is still the official flag of the forty-ninth state. It is flown just below the Stars and Stripes, and forever will symbolize the strength, courage, and beauty that the people of Alaska find in their state.

Opposite: Alaska's Bicentennial stamp shows the flag designed by Benny Benson in 1926.

Lay of the Land

LAST FRONTIER

There is a story that when Alaska became a state, a jealous Texan swore he would build a pipeline to Alaska and melt it down to the size of Delaware.

This story illustrates one of the many misunderstandings about Alaska—that great 506,400-square-mile (1,518,770-square-kilometer) sub-continent that is looked upon by many as our last frontier.

The myth that Alaska could be "melted down" dies hard. Some people still think of it as a wilderness largely covered with ice and inhabited by Eskimos who live in ice houses.

In truth, Alaska is so incredibly vast that it includes some of all those things plus a great many more.

Someone jokingly has said that a new definition of *claustrophobia* is "how an Alaskan feels in the heart of Texas." Another expert, in trying to show the magnitude of Alaska, boasted, "Take all the tall tales you've heard about Texas, multiply by ten, and you have a fairly good starting point in a yarn that nobody will believe because it's too close to the truth."

The sheer immensity of this state staggers the imagination. Alaska stretches across more meridians of longitude than the forty-eight contiguous states. Alaska is as large as the three next-largest states—Texas, California, and Montana—all rolled into one. In fact, it is one fifth as large as all the rest of the states put together.

Here the United States "touches fingers with Siberia." The mainlands of Russia and the United States are only fifty miles (eighty kilometers) apart, separated by the Bering Strait. The two nations come even closer together—less than three miles (about five kilometers) away—where Little Diomede Island (United States) nearly touches Big Diomede Island (Russia). There the two countries are actually in view of one another.

Opposite: Mt. McKinley, the highest mountain in the United States.

Alaska stretches so far to the west in the long finger of the Aleutian Islands that the International Date Line had to be bent out of shape westward to keep this part of the United States from being in an entirely different day from the rest of the country. As it is, Alaska is the only state where its legislators represent four different time zones.

Parts of Alaska are as far west as New Zealand. Anchorage, in the middle of Alaska's spread from east to west, is in the same meridian and time zone as Honolulu, Hawaii. Alaska is the only state of the United States that enters the Eastern Hemisphere.

OCEAN AND SEAS

Surrounding Alaska on all but one side are two oceans and a vast sea, giving this state the longest coastline of any of the states. In fact, if the coastlines of all of its peninsulas and islands are considered, Alaska has a longer coastline, 33,904 miles (54,563 kilometers), than all the other forty-nine states together.

Its position amid oceans and seas, of course, makes most of Alaska a peninsula, bounded by the Arctic Ocean to the north, the Bering Sea to the west, and the mighty Pacific Ocean on the southwest, south, and southeast. This peninsula, stretching away from the rest of North America, forms the northwest corner of the continent. One of the world's largest peninsulas, it is partly shared with Canada on the east.

The seas indent the shores of the main peninsula to form other peninsulas, which contribute some of the most outstanding features to Alaska's outline.

Most notable of these is the Alaska Peninsula. The peninsula itself is 550 miles (885 kilometers) long, before the spectacular chain of islands reaches toward Asia.

Another of Alaska's large peninsulas is Seward, in which a number of smaller eastern states could be swallowed up. The Kenai Peninsula, less extensive than Seward, is about the size of the state of Maryland.

12

Part of Alaska's ocean heritage, many islands lie along the fringes of the state. Much of southeastern Alaska is made up of the Alexander Archipelago of eleven hundred islands, including Baranof, Chichagof, Kuiu, Prince of Wales, Admiralty, and Revillagigedo islands. Continuing up the coast are the islands of Prince William Sound, then Afognak Island and Kodiak Island. The Semidi and Shumagin groups border the Alaska Peninsula. Beginning with Unimak and Unalaska, the Aleutian Islands pursue their bleak and windswept course in a long arc that encloses the Bering Sea. Included in the Aleutian chain are whole archipelagoes, such as the Fox, Near, Andreanof, and Rat islands.

Appearing to be adrift in the bitter and forbidding reaches of the Bering Sea are the Pribilof Islands, and Nunivak, St. Matthew, and St. Lawrence islands.

SIX DIVISIONS OF ALASKA

Geographers usually divide Alaska into six great, loosely defined sections. The southeastern section, a narrow mainland strip plus offshore islands, is sometimes called the Panhandle. It stretches down the Pacific coast as if reaching out to make contact with the rest of the United States, not too far to the south.

That land of inlets and islands fronting on the Gulf of Alaska and sheltered from the bitter north by the Alaska Range is called the Central Pacific Rim. It includes Prince William Sound, Cook Inlet, and the Kenai Peninsula.

Alaska's tremendous Interior region extends from the Alaska Range to the Brooks Range on the north and from the Canadian border on the east to the Bering Sea to the west. Here it meets the Western Approaches region, including Seward Peninsula, Norton Sound Area, Yukon-Kuskokwim Delta, Bristol Bay region, and numerous coastal islands.

To the north is the whole vast third of Alaska included in the Arctic region, well within the Arctic Circle.

Longest and narrowest of the six regions is Southwestern Alaska, including the Alaska Peninsula and the Aleutian and Kodiak islands.

"BRING ME MEN TO MATCH MY MOUNTAINS"

The tallest mountains in the world are not found in the Himalayas but in Alaska. Mt. Everest may be the highest mountain in the world, but Mt. McKinley is the tallest. No other mountain rises so high from base to peak. In the Himalayas, the surrounding land is much higher, so that Mt. Everest does not thrust itself so loftily above its base.

Mt. McKinley is a mighty Alaskan monarch. The Indians of the region have a legend that a warrior with magic powers created the mighty mountain from an ocean wave as a shield to protect him from the spear of an enemy. When he was finished with it, he threw the shield on the ground, where it looms today as the highest mountain in the United States—20,320 feet (6,193 meters)—and also the highest point on the North American continent.

Denali, "The Great One," or "Home of the Sun," is the Indian name for Mt. McKinley. It is part of the mammoth Alaska Mountain Range, one of the state's three vast primary mountain systems. The others are the Brooks Range in the north and the Pacific Range. Many separate divisions of these ranges can be classed as ranges in themselves, bearing identifying names of their own.

Lesser mountain ranges may be found throughout the state. These include the Aleutian Mountains. Where this range marches out to sea, the tops of the drowned Aleutian chain have become islands.

Chugach Mountains, Wrangell Mountains, St. Elias Mountains, and Kuskokwim Mountains are all well-known subordinate ranges. To this list could be added other mountain systems, including Romanzof, Franklin, Philip Smith, Talkeetna, Endicott, Schwatka, Baird, De Long, White, Kilbuk, and others. The Fairweather Range is known as the place where glaciers are born.

Many of Alaska's mountains are of volcanic origin. The Aleutian chain forms the longest and straightest single line of volcanoes in the

14

world. Some of Alaska's volcanoes are currently inactive, but they must be considered sleeping giants. In addition to the dormant peaks, Alaska has a large proportion of all the active volcanoes of the United States. In the Mt. Katmai region are more active volcanoes than in any other place of equal size in the world.

Mt. Shishaldin on Unimak Island has a unique trick, a spectacle hardly to be believed unless seen. This inveterate "smoker" blows smoke rings several hundred feet in diameter, as if puffed out by some tranquil giant.

Hikers in the Mt. Katmai region, where there are more active volcanoes than in any other place of equal size in the world.

ICE THAT BARKS LIKE A DOG: THE GLACIERS

In addition to the mountains, a spectacular feature of Alaska is the glaciers. Glaciers have been shaping and reshaping the mountains and valleys of Alaska for hundreds of thousands of years. Alaska, of course, experienced the glaciers of the various glacial ages that covered much of the northern half of the continent. Oddly enough, however, in a period when much of New England was buried, central Alaska was free of ice, yet permanently frozen.

Although the glaciers have gone from the rest of the United States, except for a few small ones on high mountains, in Alaska there still remains the largest amount of glacier ice outside Greenland and the polar ice caps. Giant Malaspina Glacier alone, near Yakutat, is a mass of ice larger than the whole state of Rhode Island.

Malaspina Glacier is a piedmont (fan-shaped) type of glacier. One of the two types of glaciers (continental glaciers and valley glaciers), this is formed by the merging of several valley glaciers. The valley, or Alpine, glacier is a river of ice that winds down the valleys from permanent snowfields, such as Taku and Mendenhall glaciers.

Glaciers are formed by the tremendous snows of the region. When more snow falls during the winter than can be melted during the summer, it begins to pile up on the mountains and in the valleys. As the weight of many seasons of snow presses down, the snow is changed to ice and begins to push down the valley propelled by its own weight—shoving everything in its path before it. The rate of flow ranges from 1 foot (.3 meter) to as much as 60 feet (18 meters) per day.

This flow is countered by the melting of the forward edge of the glacier. When more melts off the forward edge than is replaced by the flow, the glacier is said to be receding. This is generally due to a warming of the climate. The advance and retreat of glaciers is an indicator of climate change. In general, the glaciers of North America are receding, indicating a gradual warming of the climate.

As recently as historic times, probably about A.D. 1700, Glacier Bay was completely covered with an ice cap 3,000 feet (914 meters) thick. Today, the waters of the bay are ice free except for icebergs

Glaciers have been shaping and reshaping the mountains and valleys of Alaska for hundreds of thousands of years. In Alaska there remains the largest amount of glacier ice outside Greenland and the polar ice caps.
Left: Mendenhall Glacier icebergs.
Below: When chunks of ice drop from a glacier face into the water to form icebergs, the glacier is said to be "calving." This picture shows Riggs Glacier calving.

that break off of the glaciers that still come down to the water's edge. This has happened in the comparatively short span of 250 years.

Glacier Bay, however, still offers a most spectacular display of glaciers. In the Bay region are to be found eleven "tidal" glaciers, that is, glaciers coming to the water's edge. One of the most active glaciers on the coast is Muir. Its face rises a sheer 265 feet (81 meters) above the waterline across a 2-mile width (3.2 kilometers).

When chunks of ice drop from the glacier face into the water to form icebergs, the glacier is said to be "calving." Some of these icebergs are enormous.

A few of Alaska's glaciers are not receding. Taku is advancing about 600 feet (183 meters) per year. In 1936, Black Rapids Glacier made a spectacular advance at the rate of 25 feet (8 meters) per day and progressed several miles. Its movement was so violent that it was constantly "emitting creaks, groans, and occasional sharp barks." Such strange noises are typical of glaciers.

Where the edge of a glacier is on land rather than water, in front of it will be found its "terminal moraine," a vast accumulation of boulders, gravel, and even "intra-glacial" wood. This is called "morainal debris." The ancient glaciers of Alaska scooped up and carried with them so much material that they sometimes deposited layers of sand and gravel several hundred feet thick.

Le Conte Glacier is the southernmost tidal glacier on the Pacific coast of North America.

RIVERS AND LAKES

Few names possess the romance and legendary quality of the Yukon, one of the mighty rivers of the world. Flowing through both Canada and the United States, it has acquired a width of 3 miles (4.8 kilometers) by the time it reaches Fort Yukon, hundreds of miles from its mouth. Three of its tributaries are on the list of major rivers of the United States Geological Survey. They are the Tanana, Porcupine, and Koyukuk. The Tanana, a great river in its own right, is 800 miles long (1,287 kilometers).

The Kuskokwim River system has a drainage basin second only to the Yukon in Alaska. Both the Yukon and Kuskokwim have built extensive deltas in the Bering Sea.

Among the other rivers of Alaska listed in the geological survey are the Noatak and the Colville, the latter emptying into the bleakness of the Arctic Ocean and draining much of Alaska's enormous Arctic slope. Other large rivers of Alaska are the Susitna and Kobuk.

The Stikine River, cutting through the Coast Range, has carved canyons 1,000 feet (305 meters) in depth. It is navigable to Telegraph Creek in British Columbia.

Although there are no extremely large bodies of water in Alaska, such as the Great Lakes, the huge area of the state and the large number of rivers and smaller lakes in it combine to give Alaska the largest area of inland water in the United States—15,335 square miles (39,717 square kilometers). Lake Iliamna is Alaska's largest lake, and there are a number of other sizeable lakes at the base of the Alaska Peninsula, including Naknek, Becharof, Ugashik, and Kukaklek. Tustumena Lake on Kenai Peninsula and Selawik Lake near Kotzebue Sound are other important bodies of water.

An unusual body of water in Alaska is "self-dumping" Lake George. Water is impounded behind the glacier, forming the lake. When the water becomes too heavy, it breaks the ice dam, and Lake

Chena River

George "dumps" itself. Then the glacier advances again to make a dam, and the process is repeated. There are other self-dumping lakes, not so well known.

HOME OF PERMAFROST

Northern Alaska's location, including about a third of its area within the Arctic Circle, gives it many qualities unlike those of any other state.

About 60 percent of Alaska is included in the permafrost region. Here only 12 to 18 inches (30 to 40 centimeters) of the surface ever thaws. Below this the earth is always frozen—sometimes to a depth of 1,200 feet (366 meters). In summer, when the top layer thaws, about half of the permafrost area is under water because the melted liquid cannot sink into the frozen under-surface.

The great treeless northern area of Alaska is called the *tundra*. It is much like the northern regions all around the top of the world in North America, Asia, and Europe.

Much of the region has taken on strange polygon shapes that can be seen from the air. Cracks formed by the cold divide some portions of the land into permanent patches fifty or a hundred feet (fifteen to thirty meters) across, some of them so symmetrical they look almost like great honeycombs in aerial photographs.

To the north, the Arctic Ocean is always ready, after a short summer, to bring back its ice pack to the shores, piling up barricades (pressure ridges) of ice cakes to fantastic heights along the coasts. Over all this shimmer the playful, eerie, ever-changing shapes and fanciful colors of the aurora borealis during the winter and the most beautiful sunsets in the world during the short Arctic summer.

AL-AY-EK-SA: GREAT LAND

No state in the Union is more aptly named. Alaska, from an Aleut word *al-ay-ek-sa,* means "the great land."

Footsteps on the Land

FOUR GROUPS NATIVE TO ALASKA

According to many experts, Alaska was the first home of humankind in the Western Hemisphere. They believe that untold thousands of years ago Asia and North America were connected by land across what is now the Bering Strait. Over this land connection (isthmus) wandered men and women from Asia—during how long a period no one knows. They drifted farther and farther to the south, and some authorities feel that the entire resident population of both North and South America resulted from this migration. Gradually the land connection became submerged because of melting polar ice. The submerged section is called the Bering Sea platform.

Relatively little is known about the prehistoric peoples of Alaska. The last two thousand years have brought so many changes to the physical features of the area that few relics of ancient peoples have been unearthed. Fossil-carved ivory found along the Bering Sea coast and much material found on Kodiak Island seem to indicate that the early Alaskans had a fairly high degree of culture.

No other mainland state held such a variety of peoples. Three of these—Indian, Aleut, and Eskimo—represent distinct racial strains. Indians of Alaska are represented in two major groups: Maritime and Athapascan. These language groups had several major divisions.

THE TRAGIC ALEUT

The first people of Alaska to be met by Europeans were the Aleut. These people are related to the Eskimo but are distinct from them. The Aleut occupied parts of the Alaska Peninsula and the island chain that was named *Aleutian* in their honor.

As Russian traders and trappers came into the area, they treated the Aleut badly. Later Russian settlers dominated the Aleut people, making them hunt for furs and perform other tasks without pay-

*Early
Aleutian
Islanders*

ment. This harsh treatment almost extinguished the Aleut as a race. However, we have considerable knowledge of their way of life from the descriptions of early visitors. One visitor wrote: "Their instruments and utensils are all made with amazing beauty and the exactest [sic] symmetry; the needles with which they sew their clothes and embroidery are made of the wing bone of the gull, with a very nice cut around the thicker end, instead of an eye, to which they tie the thread so skillfully that it follows the needles without any obstruction. The thread they make of the sinews of a seal, and of all sizes, from the fineness of a hair to the strength of a moderate cord, both plaited and twisted.

". . . . Their boats are infinitely superior to those of any other. If perfect symmetry, smoothness, and proportion constitute beauty, they are beautiful . . . some of them as transparent as oiled paper."

Aleut women were noted for their basketmaking, for which they used wild rye and other grasses. Another observer records: "These baskets are made of the longest blades of grass previously dried, and for the finer work split into slips. In this process the woman uses no other instrument but . . . the nail of her forefinger, which she suffers to grow to a great length until it is as sharp as a lancet.''

TLINGIT: ''THE PEOPLE''

Occupying most of what is now southeast Alaska were the mighty Tlingit Indians. Their name is translated as ''The People.'' Writing about eighty years ago, one authority described the Tlingit as ''one of the highest and most individualistic of all American Indian cultures.''

The Tlingit were mother-centered. Tlingit chieftains inherited their possessions through their mothers, and property was passed down through the mother's descent. With this system, nephews or younger brothers were heirs, rather than sons. In this way a clan retained all of its property.

Their permanent winter homes were community houses, occupied by fifty to a hundred people. Each house was the property of a clan, all of whom were related to one another. Villages consisted of eight to fifteen houses.

Totems were carved into the supports of the house or painted on one wall inside. Originally, the Tlingit did not carve separate totem poles to be set outside the house, but other groups did this, and the Tlingits took up the practice. Totems had several different meanings. Some were used as family crests. Others served as monuments. Anyone belonging to the clan could use the clan design. Totems often told clan or tribal history. Even ''bills'' were carved on totems as a visible reminder of unpaid debts. Sometimes totems were nothing more than giant ''storybooks'' telling the mythology and tales of the people with signs and symbols. The bright colors of totems were made from crushed rock of various colors, minerals, and clam shells, mixed with fish eggs as a binder.

Some totems as high as eighty feet (twenty-four meters) have been found. Experts can ''read'' these totems almost as easily as a

Tlingit traditions are still carried on. Right: Tlingit relics at Hoonah. Below: Tlingit dancers at Klawock.

book. They are read from top to bottom. One of the favorite totem symbols was the mighty thunderbird.

Flapping of the thunderbird's wings made the thunder, according to Tlingit belief, and rain came when water spilled over from the great lake on the back of the thunderbird. The raven also was used often in totems. That wise bird was said to have placed the sun, moon, and stars in the sky for the Tlingit's use.

Tlingit legend declared that the earth rested on the post of the "old woman underneath." When she became fidgety, the earth shook and quaked. The Tlingit greeted inanimate objects, always speaking a friendly hello or good-bye to mountains. They had a "speaking acquaintance" with glaciers and other natural objects. Each boulder in a favorite fishing stream might bear a friendly name.

Proudest possessions of the Tlingit were their beautiful blankets woven from the wool of wild goats; these were used almost as modern man uses money. An uncle might offer a dowry of forty blankets to the family of his nephew's bride.

Wealth, rank, and prestige were greatly prized. A Tlingit won respect by his ability to give away or destroy large quantities of property. At feasts called *potlatches,* the host would present to his guests valuable articles such as blankets, canoes, or sheets of copper. Guests who could not return gifts of greater value lost prestige.

Their main livelihood came from the sea, and they were skillful boatmen. Their graceful canoes were hollowed from logs and made wider by soaking the wood and then forcing the sides apart with small logs. They were sometimes large enough to carry sixty persons.

Those Indians living west of the Chilkat River bore the name Chilkat—those to the east, Chilcoot. The Chilkat were the only blanket weavers of all the Tlingit. In fact, all Tlingit blankets are known as Chilkats. Chilkat blanket weaving is almost a lost art. Materials used in these blankets are sinew, yellow cedar bark, and mountain goat's wool. The wool from as many as ten goats may be required for one blanket. Three colors were used—black, from hemlock bark, blue-green from copper, and yellow from lichen. Each maker uses a different design, and the same design may stay in a family for generations as a kind of totem.

In addition to carving wood and weaving blankets, Tlingit crafts-men wove beautiful baskets of spruce roots, decorated with dyed grasses. They fashioned handsome wooden boxes and elaborate ceremonial masks.

Among the strongest and most aggressive branches of the Tlingit people were the Stikine Indians. Another mighty Tlingit branch was the Sitka.

In one of the many wars between the Sitka and the Stikine, the fable is told of the Stikine chief who complained that his people were hungry since they did not dare to go to the salmon streams and berry patches for food. He urged the Sitka chief to stop the fighting. The Sitka chief replied that the Stikine had killed ten more of his tribe than were killed by the Sitka. "Give us ten Stikine men to balance our blood-account; then and not till then will we make peace and go home."

"Very well," replied the Stikine chief, "you know my rank. You know that I am worth ten common men and more. Take me and make peace." He stepped forward, was immediately shot, and peace came once more.

In actuality, the feud between the two groups was carried on into modern times and was ended by a written treaty. A signed copy of this treaty is owned by the Alaska Historical Library and Museum.

OTHER INDIANS

The second main grouping of Alaska Indians was the Athapascan (or Tinneh), occupying the Yukon, Kuskokwim, Koyukuk, Copper, and other interior river systems, except at the mouths of the Kuskokwim, Yukon, and Copper. They were known particularly for their intricate beadwork on moose hide, which they still do. Being migratory, they had few material possessions.

About 150 years before the Russians came, some members of the Haida group from British Columbia moved northward to various islands, including Prince of Wales, which the Haida still occupy. The Haida, in the early days of Russian occupation, were distinguished

U.S. 6c

HAIDA CEREMONIAL CANOE

United States postage stamp honors Alaskan peoples.

for their prowess in war, their sea-going dugout canoes, and their venturesome sea roving.

Another migrating group in the southeastern section is the Tsimshian, which came from farther east on the mainland in British Columbia to settle on Annette Island. They were noted for their fine carvings, rattles, bentwood boxes, and mountain sheep- and goat-horn spoons. They invented the Chilkat blanket.

GENIUS OF THE ARCTIC: THE ESKIMO

Eskimo of Alaska are among the most versatile people of North America. They are certainly one of the most interesting people found within the continental limits of the United States.

Experts feel that the Eskimo made up the last wave of the many waves of peoples that filtered across the Bering Strait to populate the Americas. Ranging over 200,000 square miles (about 520,000 square kilometers) of Alaska territory, throughout historical times, the Eskimo have occupied the coasts of the Bering Sea and Arctic Ocean and the islands in those waters, as well as large reaches of the interior, especially up such rivers as the Yukon and the Kuskokwim.

Contrary to the usual notion, early explorers did not find the Eskimo living in ice houses. The word *igloo* simply means "building." The permanent winter home of the Eskimo was a dugout house, much like the sod houses of the Great Plains states. If a snow igloo was built, it was for temporary shelter when the Eskimo could not return to his regular home for a night or two.

The organization of Eskimo life has been the most unusual among the peoples of the United States. There were no "tribes" and no "chief" in the Indian sense. An outstanding Eskimo would be only the "first among equals." Government was simply a "free accord of free people."

All who were able did as much work as possible in the life-and-death struggle for food and clothing. This hard work by all was a desperate necessity in the harsh region where the Eskimo lived. When game was killed, it became the property of the community. Each family took what it needed when huge meat supplies, such as whales, were captured. When an Eskimo boy made his first kill, there was a great feast and much rejoicing.

The Eskimo have no written language. During the years since Europeans first came into contact with them, only a comparatively few Europeans have ever learned to speak the Eskimo language.

Plundering by newcomers lends a sad note to the story of the Eskimo. The whalers were particularly unscrupulous in dealing with Eskimo peoples.

The Eskimo suffered greatly from European diseases. Tuberculosis was especially devastating.

Eskimo and Indian peoples usually are considered to be distantly related, coming from the same racial stock, but some authorities doubt this. The Eskimo and Indians in Alaska feared each other.

An interesting branch of the Eskimo were the Chugachamint people. They lived in the Chugach Mountain region, practically surrounded by hostile Indians. The village of Chugach was inhabited by Chugachamints until March 27, 1964, when an earthquake destroyed their town. Then they moved to Tatetlik, though the Chugach name lives on in their region.

Eskimo artists and craftsmen have left evidence of their skills from ancient times, and modern-day Eskimo artists are renowned for their creativity. The Eskimo were noted for their skill in carving ivory ornaments and statuary from walrus tusks. The light and seaworthy *umiak,* a boat made of walrus skins, was a good example of their craftsmanship. Eskimo people were familiar with iron working in early times but lost the art in later days.

Eskimo arts and crafts at Nome.

"ENQUIRE WHERE THE AMERICAN COAST BEGINS"

Strangely enough, the modern history of northwestern America begins with Czar Peter the Great of Russia. That mighty monarch sent Vitus Bering, a Dane who served with the Russian navy, to the coast of Siberia. Bering was to explore the coast of Asia, find where the coast of North America began, and explore and map the North American coast. In 1728 Bering found the strait now named for him, but did not come to the mainland of North America until 1741. The life and work of this extraordinary explorer are taken up in more detail later.

Bering is usally called the discoverer of Alaska, but it is probable that a Russian explorer, Michael Gvozdev, touched Diomede Island, and possibly the North American mainland, as early as 1732. He and his expedition sailed along the shores of what they thought was an island for several days. Finally Gvozdev concluded it must be a continent. This was probably in the region of Norton Sound and the shoals of the Yukon River.

After the expeditions of Gvozdev and Bering, Russian fur traders visited the North American coasts more and more frequently. Between 1743 and 1799, they plundered Alaska of more than two hundred thousand skins of the beautiful sea otter, nearly driving to extinction that prized and charming animal. At this time, hunters from other countries also were able to trade for furs with the residents of the land.

Russian headquarters of a temporary sort had been set up on the island of Unalaska. In 1762 the Aleut peoples of Umnak and Unalaska rose up against the cruelties of the Russians; they captured and destroyed four Russian ships and killed a number of Russian hunters. However, the revolt was put down. The Russian leader, Feodor Soloviev, killed possibly as many as three thousand Aleut for revenge. The gentle Aleut spirit was so broken by this cruelty that the Aleuts never again rose against their harsh Russian masters.

The first permanent European settlement in what is now Alaska was the trading headquarters established by the Russians at Kodiak in 1784.

30

During the fur period, exploring and mapping were being carried out by Russian, Spanish, French, and English navigators. From 1774 to 1794 several Spanish expeditions went out from the Spanish settlements in southwestern North America, including those of Bodega y Quadra. In 1790 Spanish Lieutenant Salvador Fidalgo named a bay Puerto de Valdes. There was one French expedition under La Pérouse and another under Roquefeuil.

The most famous explorer of them all was the English navigator, James Cook. In 1778 Captain Cook sailed up the waterway that has been named Cook Inlet in his honor. There was great excitement on board. For more than two hundred years the monarchs of Europe had sent their ablest men to find a "Northwest Passage" between Europe and the riches of the Orient. Now it appeared that this inlet might be the long-sought passageway. Cook's great disappointment can be imagined as he reached the end of navigation and sadly named those waters "Turn-again Arm"—the spot where he was forced to turn once again from hope of the great discovery. That name of disappointment remains on maps today.

During this expedition Captain Cook sailed into the Arctic Ocean. If he had only known, and if the ice floes had not turned him away once more, here was the true Northwest Passage that men had sought for so long.

Another famed English explorer, George Vancouver, explored the coast in 1791, 1792, and 1794. One of his captains described the mountains of the mainland north of the Stikine River as "uncommonly awful and horribly magnificent."

THE PARIS OF THE NORTH?

Recognizing the need for more formal organization of his domains in Alaska, Czar Paul I granted exclusive authority in the region to the Russian-American Company. Siberian merchant Alexander Baranof was selected by the company to go to Kodiak and direct the company operations at the scene. From that time almost until his death, he ruled his vast territory like a little czar.

This was the beginning of one of the extraordinary episodes of history—the flowering of a remote and little-known portion of the world into a unique civilization.

The beginning, however, was not easy. When the fur supply of the Aleutians seemed about exhausted, Baranof founded what he hoped would become his capital in the more rewarding region and pleasanter climate of what is now Alaska's southeast. In 1799, on Baranof Island, he established Redoubt (Fort) St. Michael, about 6 miles (9.7 kilometers) north of what is now Sitka. Leaving the settlement in charge of an assistant, he returned for a time to Kodiak.

The fierce Sitka branch of the Tlingit was entirely different from the yielding Aleut. They were shrewd bargainers and dangerous enemies. The village of the Sitka, near Baranof's new settlement, had already become an established port of call for Yankee traders on the China run. Frequently, the Yankees found themselves "on the short end of the trade." In 1802 the Sitka attacked Fort St. Michael and wiped out most of the Russians and the Aleut helpers they had brought to Baranof Island. Women and children were enslaved.

It took Baranof two years at Kodiak to muster enough strength to consider retaking his former location. In 1804, with a force of about 150 Russian hunters, he set out for the Indian village of Sitka. Accompanying him on the long voyage, in their frail *bidarkas* (boats made of skin), were 800 Aleut slaves. The *Neva,* a Russian ship that was in port, attempted to help Baranof overcome the Sitka.

Strongly fortified behind thick log walls, the Sitka withstood even the heavy guns of the ship. Baranof himself led an attack which was repulsed by murderous fire from the Sitka; the Russians were fortunate to regain their ships with only ten men killed and twenty-six wounded. Baranof himself was among the wounded. However, after a siege of several days, the Indians ran out of ammunition and fled over the mountain to the northeast side of the island. There they set up a new fort.

Shortly after the Battle of Sitka, the Russians chose the site of the Sitka Indian village for their new settlement. They called it New Archangel but it soon came to be known as Sitka, as it still is today. This was Alaska's first capital. A fortified headquarters building was

Rare 1860s watercolor of Sitka from the southwest is thought to have been painted by a Russian naval officer. Unfortunately, there is no record of his name.

built, and within a year, a total of eight substantial buildings had been erected. The leader of the Russian-American Company ruled a growing empire. A flour and lumber mill and tannery were established, along with a blacksmith shop. Trade was carried on with areas as far away as Lower California and Hawaii, but distant China offered the finest market for Alaska's furs.

Somehow the legend has grown that faraway Sitka was one of the most brilliant cultural centers of the Western Hemisphere. The story is told that sailors from all over the world, anchoring in Sitka harbor after their tremendously long voyages, described Sitka as the "Paris of the North." It was said that the world's adventurers thronged the streets, and that many formal balls gave Russian women an opportunity to show off their beautiful evening gowns and the men their handsome uniforms.

The legend that some of the bells in remote California's missions were cast in Sitka is one of the hardest to die. Much as we might like to believe these romantic stories, most of them are exaggerations or downright fabrications.

Nevertheless, at its height, Russian Sitka really was a surprising metropolis of the wilderness. It boasted an astronomical observatory, a library, a forty-bed hospital, doctors, druggists, and a school. The buildings of old Sitka were striking, with their squared log sides washed in bright yellow ochre and topped by red metal roofs. The first St. Michael's Cathedral, completed in 1848, was noted throughout the world for its religious treasures.

Meanwhile, Baranof was expanding his domain, creating outposts in other parts of Alaska including Cook Inlet, Prince William Sound, Bristol Bay, and the Pribilofs. Most astonishing of all to most Americans is the fact that Russian Fort Ross was established just north of San Francisco Bay and flourished for some time as a Russian outpost.

Because Baranof's power began to trouble the Russian leaders, in 1818 he was dismissed and sent home in the custody of the Russian navy. He died at sea on the Indian Ocean during the long voyage home to Russia. The Russians quickly moved to tighten their hold on this rich land. They ordered the whole coast north of 54° 40′ closed to other nations, except for trade.

Neither England nor the United States paid much attention to this decree, however. By 1824 the United States was able to sign an agreement with Russia for trading privileges in the area, throughout a ten-year period. Another favorable trade treaty was also signed with England.

As the Russian position at Sitka was being consolidated, new life was stirring in other parts of Alaska. In 1826 the English explorer Beechey was the first European to see the top of North America. The Eskimo called it Nuwuk (The Point); Beechey renamed it Point Barrow in honor of Sir John Barrow. In 1834, at the present site of Wrangell, the Russians built Redoubt St. Dionysius to help guard against the growing fur-trade competition of the English Hudson's Bay Company.

In spite of this, the Hudson's Bay Company established itself in a trading post at Fort Yukon, an incredible distance across the wilderness from its headquarters. The year was 1847. Russia began to feel her hold on Alaska slipping. United States' captains operated openly in whaling and trading in Alaska waters, despite the fact that the earlier treaty for doing this had expired.

When the Civil War came to the United States, the Confederate cruiser *Shenandoah* moved to the Alaska coast to stalk Union whalers. It is a strange fact that the last gun of the Civil War was fired in the far-off waters of the Bering Sea on June 22, 1865. The *Shenandoah* did not yet know that the war was ended when it attacked a Union whaling vessel that day.

A NEW FLAG AT SITKA

Americans became better acquainted with Alaska through the Western Union Telegraph expedition to the region in the years 1865-1867. Attempts to lay a communications cable across the Atlantic had been unsuccessful up to that point. Western Union authorities had felt it might be more practical to lay a cable overland through Canada and Alaska and across the narrow Bering Strait, and then across the vastness of Siberia.

When the Atlantic cable finally succeeded, this project was abandoned, but the American cable engineers and other experts made many interesting discoveries about Alaska during their two years there. Under the leadership of Robert Kennicott, famed scientist and explorer, and Frederick Whymper, artist, the cable company provided information for the first maps of the interior and valuable data on the natural resources of the country. On his death, Kennicott was succeeded by the renowned William H. Dall. Later, Whymper wrote his book *Travels in Alaska* to give the average man his first real information about that region. Dall published *Alaska and Its Resources* in 1870, and dedicated the book to Kennicott.

The stage was set for one of those "lucky" combinations of circumstances through which the United States has acquired so much of its territory. Under instructions from his government, the Russian Minister to the United States, Baron Edouard von Stoeckel, began to urge the American government to buy Alaska. This persuasive early-day Russian lobbyist spent $200,000 lobbying for the sale. As one writer has said, "The mystery is not why Russia wished to sell but why the United States wanted to buy." Russia was afraid

Emmanuel Leutz's painting shows Secretary of State Seward holding the pen, inviting the Russian diplomat, standing at the globe, to sign the Alaska purchase agreement.

that if she did not sell, she would lose Alaska to the English, who would simply take it over. On the other hand, most Americans thought of Alaska as barren and worthless.

The American Secretary of State, William H. Seward, had greater vision than most of his countrymen. Through his foresight, a treaty of purchase was negotiated and signed on March 30, 1867. In this treaty, Russia agreed to cede all of Russian America to the United States for $7,200,000.

Most Americans of the day were indignant. They called Alaska "Seward's Folly" or "Seward's Icebox." Only now are we beginning to get a true picture of the magnificent contribution Seward made to his country when he bought this land at the ridiculously low figure of two cents per acre (five cents per hectare).

In solemn ceremonies on October 18, 1867, the Russian flag was lowered from the pole in front of Government House on the hill at Sitka. The faces of the Russian residents were somber. Princess Maksoutof, whose husband was the last Russian governor, was said to have wept as she watched the Russian flag fall on the soldiers' bayonets. Two American generals and three navy captains, accompanied by two hundred enlisted men and sixty civilians, stood and cheered as the American flag officially rose over Alaska.

A new day had dawned for Alaska.

36

Yesterday and Today

LAWLESS OBLIVION

Alaska's new day was a long time coming.

Someone has said that "three decades of complete oblivion for Alaska" followed the United States purchase. Actually, there were seventeen years of neglect. Alaska became a "District" of the United States in 1884, but almost no provisions were made for civil government or law and order.

After sixty-six years of domination of a vast Alaskan empire, the Russian-American Company in 1867 sold its business to a new Alaska Company headed by an American, H.M. Hutchinson. The Russians were supposed to have been guaranteed rights of citizenship if they wished to stay, and a few indicated that they wanted to remain in their homes, but for one cause or another most of them soon left in disgust.

During the period between 1867 and 1884 a degree of anarchy prevailed in Alaska, with a seemingly callous disregard by the government at Washington and the military authorities. Lynching of so-called witches, and other crimes, flourished, with no civil authority to put a stop to them.

In 1880 two prospectors, Dick Harris and Joe Juneau, began to search the mountainsides and streambeds in the area of the Gastineau Channel. A large gold lode was discovered in Silver Bow Basin near the headwaters of Gold Creek. Before a year had passed, more than a hundred gold seekers were camping where Juneau is today, marking the founding of what was to become, in 1906, Alaska's capital city.

Harris and Juneau argued mightily about which of them would have the honor of naming the town. It had been called Thunder Creek (Indian), Pilzberg, Rockwell, and Harrisburgh. Finally at a meeting of the miners in 1882, it was decided to call the new community Juneau, with the district to be named Harris.

Joe Juneau realized a fortune from his holdings, but he was so afraid he would not live long enough to spend all his money that he squandered his wealth and finally died penniless in Dawson during the Klondike stampede.

METLAKATLA: A TRIUMPH OF RELIGION

Under the direction of a Scottish lay minister, a remarkable development began in Alaska in 1887. A group of Tsimshian Indians from British Columbia came to Annette Island with a missionary, the Reverend William Duncan.

They called their new village Metlakatla, in honor of their former home. Missionary Duncan had been working with the Tsimshian Indians in Metlakatla, British Columbia, since 1857. He had helped them to create a model community but had been relieved of his position by the British leaders of his missionary body. When he left Canada in 1887, 820 of his devoted followers went with him to Annette Island, where he named his settlement New Metlakatla.

Here, under his guidance, they produced another model community. Lots were assigned to individuals, streets were laid out, and comfortable houses were built. A sawmill, salmon cannery, school, and church were created. Through Duncan's remarkable efforts, Congress, in 1891, set aside Annette Island as a reservation for the Metlakatla Indians and gave them exclusive rights to fish in all waters within 3,000 feet (914 meters) of the island shores.

William Duncan remained in Metlakatla as an honored citizen until his death in 1918. His work was one of the bright spots in the history of Alaska of this period.

ON TO THE KLONDIKE!

Gold had been discovered in the Klondike region of Canada's Yukon in 1896. In 1897 the steamer *Portland* sailed into Seattle harbor with a ton of Klondike gold, and the rush was on. Suddenly great numbers of people, mostly American, determined to get the riches of the Klondike, regardless of the consequences. At Skagway, there

38

was only one cabin on the beach when the first swarms of gold hunters, between ten and twenty thousand, began to arrive. Almost overnight Skagway sprang into being with a transient population of fifteen thousand.

Skagway was the nearest gateway to the interior of the Klondike. However, it had neither supplies nor facilities. Many of the adventurers were arriving with hardly more than the clothes on their backs and no idea of the difficulties or dangers of traveling into the interior and prospecting for gold in that severe land.

There were two passes—Chilkoot and White—from Skagway through the coastal mountains to the Klondike. Both were bad. Most prospectors chose Chilkoot Pass. Wise Swiss mountaineers would have classified this pass as a dangerous mountain climb. Yet in 1898, about twenty-two thousand eager, inexperienced men crossed over it on their way to hoped-for gold. Sometimes there were so many in line that they were almost touching one another for miles. In April, a terrible avalanche buried most of the men who happened to be climbing the pass at the time.

Other prospectors tried to reach Canada's gold by a route over Valdez Glacier, a treacherous sheet of solid ice. Even in the winter of 1898, thirty-five hundred prospectors crossed Valdez Glacier. Captain W.R. Abercrombie describes his experiences in crossing: "The wind was blowing a hurricane, accompanied by gusts of sleet and snow [that] coated men and beasts with an armour of ice. . . . The only thing to do was to simply drift with the blizzard. Had the wind blown into the pass from the right or left the expedition would have simply drifted out onto the great glacial fields. . . . After some five or six hours travel in the howling storm, where it was impossible to hear or see a comrade, a high and rocky cliff was finally rounded and the expedition beheld the most beautiful sight I ever witnessed.

"The change was almost magical. Two yards after passing behind the shelter of this rocky cliff there was a perfect haven of rest and sunshine, while out of the pass rushed the howing storm like the water out of the nozzle of a fire hose. . . . I had now successfully crossed the Valdez Glacier at a season of the year when it was universally conceded to be impassable."

Another three thousand prospectors crossed Valdez Glacier during the summer. At both Skagway and Valdez many failed to make it. No one can be certain how many were left in roadside graves, often beside the carcasses of their fallen horses.

ON TO NOME!

The next gold fever hit in Alaska itself. In 1899 gold was found on the beaches at Nome. This was unlike almost any other strike in history. Here the gold was right on the beach. Even more strangely, it lay in the stretch of the beach between high and low tides, so that the gold-bearing sands were exposed only as the tide went out.

All that was necessary to become rich was to be able to wash enough of the golden treasure out of the loose sand. Even more important, the General Land Office decreed that no claims could be staked below the usual level of high tide. The wealth of Nome's beaches simply awaited anyone who could pan it out of the sand.

No wonder Nome became the historic scene of one of the world's most notorious gold rushes. Before the run was over, it was estimated that as many as forty thousand gold-mad men and women struggled for the fabulous riches of Nome's Gold Beach.

Of course, only a fortunate few of the many thousands could be successful. By July it was reported that there were already ten thousand people on the sands of Nome. Most of them had possessed only enough money to buy a one-way passage. Tents were pitched for three miles (nearly five kilometers) along the beach in rows twenty deep. Gold hunters kept swarming in at a daily rate of almost a thousand. Soon there was not even tent room. Even women and children were sleeping unprotected on the damp beaches.

Nome as a city actually did not exist then, although its population had probably passed twenty thousand. When boats arrived with

Opposite: Travel in Alaska still has its hazards and thrills (top) and still can be much the same as in pioneer days (bottom).

freight, unprotected supplies were dumped on the beach. There was no provision for sanitation, and most wells were contaminated. Typhoid, lawlessness, and famine stalked the deluded multitude.

As their dream of wealth failed them, some were taken back to southern west-coast ports by revenue cutters. Others, however, drifted off to look for gold elsewhere; many found work of one kind or another, such as railroad building. Many found only a lonely grave.

SOME MORE DISCOVERIES

A gold discovery by Felix Pedro in the interior led to the birth of Fairbanks in 1902. Since the gold was buried deep and required expensive equipment to work, Fairbanks never experienced the kind of rush that plagued Nome. Its growth and development were more orderly. Herb E. Willson, one of the prospectors, wrote: "A meeting of the early stampeders was held on newly discovered Pedro Creek, and there we appointed a recorder and named the place Fairbanks, after the senator who later became vice president of the United States."

Another "discovery" of importance took place in 1902. It seems hard to realize that a natural feature as prominent as Mt. McKinley, discovered in 1896 by W.A. Dickey, was not touched by European explorers until the twentieth century. In 1902 Alfred H. Brooks and D.L. Reaburn were the first Europeans to set foot on the slopes of that mighty mountain.

In 1903 a dispute with Canada over the boundary line to the southeast was settled in favor of the United States by a committee of arbitrators.

As prospectors spread out over more and more of the countryside, mineral discoveries continued. Placer gold was found along the Kautishna River in 1905.

The year 1906 saw slightly more government attention turned toward Alaska and its problems. Congress passed a fisheries bill in an effort to conserve the diminishing supply of salmon, and the government was moved from its historic, long-time post at Sitka to Juneau in that year.

In 1912 the first territorial government in Alaska was organized when Congress passed a second Organic Act, providing for the first elected legislature in Alaska. Alaska became a territory, with a voteless delegate in Congress.

"PRELUDE TO HELL"

On June 6, 1912, with a terrifying rumble, the top of Mount Katmai suddenly blew apart. Much of the mountain was almost instantly turned to ash, with a roar heard 750 miles (1,200 kilometers) away. The ash was so thick that daylight turned to almost total darkness for 100 miles (161 kilometers) around.

The green island of Kodiak, 100 miles (161 kilometers) away, became a dusty, gray desert. People on the island had to shovel ashes off their roofs to keep them from collapsing. For five days, violent earthquakes shook the region. On June 8, one observer wrote, "A mountain has burst near here, so that we are covered with ashes, in some places 10 feet deep (3 meters).... Night and day we light lamps. In a word it is terrible, and we are expecting death any moment, and we have no water.... Here are darkness and hell, thunder and noise. The earth is trembling."

The explosion of Katmai is considered one of the two or three most violent volcanic eruptions in history. Only the holocaust that destroyed Mt. Krakatoa in the East Indies is known to have been worse. The great cloud of dust from Katmai rose into the air and circled the world, cooling the weather all over the Northern Hemisphere, dimming the sun, and in most areas creating sunsets of unparalleled magnificence. Strangely, on the part of Mt. Katmai that was left, the side away from the wind was almost completely undamaged by the dust.

Forty square miles (104 square kilometers) of a nearby valley were "buried in a river of incandescent sand" up to 700 feet (213 meters) deep. The National Geographic Society sent a famous expedition to explore this valley. They wrote that innumerable cracks and vents had been torn in the valley floor. It looked as if "all the steam engines in the world, assembled together, had popped their safety valves at once and were letting off surplus steam in concert."

Because of the multitude of steam vents, they gave this region its now famous name—the "Valley of Ten Thousand Smokes." Some steam jetted as high as 1,000 feet (305 meters). Brightly colored mud painted much of the area. At the present time, however, the valley has almost ceased to live up to its name, with practically no steam visible.

The eruption of Mt. Katmai had a weird aftereffect on Kodiak Island's famous bears. Observers noted that many of the bears were shambling about very nearly naked. Mixed with rainwater, the volcanic ash that covered them had formed a dilute sulphuric acid. This had eaten their fur away and left the animals without protection.

If this eruption had occurred in a heavily populated area, the damage to property and loss of life would have been immeasurable. Out of the tiny population, two hundred lives were lost.

CIVILIZATION ADVANCES

In 1914 President Woodrow Wilson signed the Alaska railroad bill, and the route for a much-talked-of railroad from the coast at Seward to the interior was chosen. Not long afterward, a tent village for construction workers sprang up along the proposed right of way. This marked the beginning of Alaska's metropolis, Anchorage.

Nine years later, the tremendous construction job was completed. On July 15, 1923, President Harding, accompanied by Secretary of the Interior Herbert Hoover, drove a golden spike at the north end of the Tanana River Bridge, marking completion of the road to Fairbanks.

The diphtheria epidemic at Nome in 1925 focused world attention on what was then considered a typical Alaskan epic. Serum was

44

Sled dogs like those pictured here were used to carry diptheria serum from Nenana to Nome during the epidemic in 1925.

available at Nenana, but this was 650 miles (1,046 kilometers) from Nome, and only dogsled transportation was available. Over the snowy countryside glided the lifesaving supplies, passed from one relay of dog teams to another. Lead dog on the last team was Balto. As Balto mushed down the street of Nome on the last leg of that historic journey, he became one of the most famous canine heroes of all time. Newspapers blazoned the story around the world, and a monument was erected in Balto's honor in faraway Central Park in New York City. Leonard Seppala says, however, that Balto was only a "newspaper hero." Togo, who led his team across a treacherous 200-mile (322-kilometer) stretch, the longest run of all, should have had hero's honors.

In 1935 one of the world's renowned men, the humorist, writer, and motion-picture star Will Rogers, flew into Juneau in the plane of his friend, the almost equally famous flier, Wiley Post. At Juneau, his friend Rex Beach asked Rogers if he felt any fear of flying into the north country. "Not with ol' Wiley," Will assured him. "He's the most careful pilot I ever knew. Amelia Earhart told me she considered him the finest flier in the world."

From Juneau, they flew to Anchorage and Fairbanks. When they left Fairbanks, against the advice of local fliers, their radio warned of heavy fog at their destination, Barrow. They managed to land their pontoon plane on Walakpa Lagoon, sixteen miles (twenty-six kilometers) southwest of Barrow. When they took off again, the plane crashed, as the Eskimo family of Clare Okpeasha looked on in horror. When Okpeasha reached Barrow to get help, he said in broken English, "One man big, have tall boots. Other man short, have sore eye, rag over eye." Wiley Post wore a patch over one eye.

And in this way the world learned it had lost two of its most beloved figures at the place where North America ends.

The year 1935 saw another, much happier, event take place in Alaska.

During the Great Depression that began in 1929, the federal government had been looking for a place to relocate people, especially farmers who had suffered from drought and depression. They chose Alaska's Matanuska Valley for this pioneering, colonizing venture.

It was hard going for the two hundred Midwest families who decided to brave the trip. Land had to be cleared, houses built, and temporary shelters endured. Even with the help of the government and modern earthmoving and farming equipment, some families became discouraged and left. Most of those pioneers who remained eventually built a good new life.

The late 1930s saw Alaska forecasting events to come in the Pacific. Beginning in 1930, Japanese fishermen had been operating in the Pacific. They had "floating canneries," where salmon were completely processed at sea. By 1937, with the use of huge nets and other devices, these floating factories had succeeded in blocking off a large part of the salmon run. Alaska fishermen temporarily "solved" this problem by arming themselves with high-powered rifles to repel the Japanese fishermen.

WAR AND PEACE

During World War II the Japanese once again made threats in Alaskan waters, but this time in a way that menaced the whole

46

United States. Japanese forces managed to invade the Aleutian Islands and occupy Agattu, Attu, and Kiska. This was the only territory of the Continental United States they held during the war. Alaska defense headquarters were based at Anchorage, and there was a new naval base at Dutch Harbor.

By 1943, the Japanese had managed to buffer their defenses with a string of island bases extending from the Solomon Islands to the North Pacific. When the United States went on the offensive, the Aleutian end of this island fortress chain was among the first to feel America's new power. Operating in the bleak and barren reaches of the Aleutians, United States forces recaptured the three islands in 1943.

After the war, because of its strategic location, Alaska became one of the world's greatest fortresses, with growing army, navy, and air force bases in many areas. Elmendorf Air Base, headquarters of the Alaskan Command, Fort Richardson at Anchorage, Fort Wainwright and Eielson air bases near Fairbanks, and the navy installations at Kodiak and Adak ranked among the leading military centers.

One of the most remarkable defense systems ever conceived is the D.E.W. Line, "Distant Early Warning," system designed to give the earliest possible warning to the United States in the event of missile or manned aircraft attack from the northwest. The various stations of the D.E.W. Line, with their intricate detection mechanisms, were stretched across Alaska and parts of Canada like some strange successor to the great wall of China. Building this complex system in the frozen wilds will undoubtedly be classed among the major scientific and engineering achievements of its day.

JOY AND SORROW

A 15-foot (4.6-meter) golden star sailed into the air, hoisted by a giant weather balloon; 49 enormous bonfires blazed; sirens howled and bells rang out; citizens of Fairbanks even tried to turn the Chena River gold to symbolize the gold of Alaska, but through some error it turned green instead. Parties and festivities went on through the daylit night. Alaskans were celebrating a day that had been ninety-one years in coming.

In the early 1950s Alaskans began to agitate for statehood in earnest. June 30, 1958, saw their dreams come true when Congress passed a bill admitting Alaska to statehood. The news was flashed to Alaska to set off the celebration there.

On January 3, 1959, President Dwight D. Eisenhower issued a proclamation admitting Alaska as the 49th state, the first addition to the roster since 1912. Alaska's first United States senators, Ernest Gruening and E.L. Bartlett, were among the proud and happy onlookers at the ceremony. First state governor was William Allen Egan.

Since statehood, the most compelling event in Alaska history interrupted the peaceful reverence of Good Friday, March 27, 1964. Among the residents of Anchorage that day was Sister Phillias, who lay in her bed on the tenth floor at Providence Hospital after an operation. She recalled: "Suddenly the whole building was moving. My flowers tumbled off the table and the vase broke. The table and the chair slid across the room and so did my bed. . . . Each time the building would sway I'd say, 'It can't hold up. The building just can't last.' Then I saw the big Thermopane glass loosen. I pulled the covers up over my head and curled up like a ball. The glass fell down on the floor but it missed my bed."

Sister Phillias did not know it at the time, but she had just been experiencing the worst earthquake ever to hit the North American continent and the second worst known to history. On the Richter scale, a measurement of the force of earthquakes, the Alaska quake of 1964 measured 8.4 to 8.6. This earthquake is thought to have released about twice the energy of the famous 1906 earthquake in San Francisco. It was centered in Prince William Sound, which is surrounded by a large proportion of Alaska's most highly developed area, including Anchorage, Seward, Valdez, and Kodiak.

Montague Island in Prince William Sound was raised as much as 60 feet (183 meters) in some places. West of the Sound, land sank from 4 to 6 feet (1.2 to 1.8 meters). In Anchorage, houses and buildings fell into yawning crevasses. When Dr. Richard Sutherland hurried to his home in the Turnagain section after the quake, his $35,000 home was gone. It had dropped out of sight. "It's a sickening feeling," he said. Fortunately, Mrs. Sutherland and the children were safe. "As soon as she heard the first sounds, she grabbed the kids and ran out of the house. A minute later the yard and the house—everything—fell into that hole."

Five children were at home in one house when the tremors boiled beneath the ground. All of them but the year-old infant had fled their house safely. The oldest boy, eleven, ran back into the trembling house and grabbed the baby. Just as he stepped from the building, the earth gave way, and they were washed away with the house in the churning water. All over the quake area similar tragedies and near tragedies occurred.

A tidal wave, called *tsunami*, was created by the earthquake and surged back against Alaska's shore with the force of many atom bombs. Adding to the destruction of the quake itself, the tsunami devastated large areas of Kodiak, Seward, Valdez, and Whittier, and the lower Kenai Peninsula, and completely destroyed several small villages. In far away Crescent City, California, the tsunami raced ashore, smashing the business center. Cars were piled on top of one another, mammoth oil tanks burst into flames, people were washed out to sea, and much other damage and loss of life occurred. Many other distant parts of the Pacific basin felt the force of the tidal wave that began with the Alaska earthquake.

In view of the severity of the disaster, the loss of life in Alaska was almost miraculously light. Only 115 were reported dead or missing. Total damage to the state of Alaska was set at nearly six hundred million dollars.

However, even after suffering this calamity, Alaskans were eager to rebuild almost before the ground stopped shaking. It was necessary to relocate the towns of Valdez and Chenega because their sites had become too unstable. In Anchorage, a buttressing project enabled the relocation of land along busy Fourth Avenue, which had slumped as much as ten feet (three meters). Permanent changes in land levels affected harbors, roads, clam beds, factory sites, and parts of other towns.

The disastrous earthquake of 1964 caused a tremendous amount of damage to the heavily populated Anchorage area. Right: A badly damaged building. Below: The north side of Fourth Avenue.

Above: The Turnagain area.
Below: The highway southeast of Anchorage.

Above: Tower, Anchorage International Airport.
Below: Railroad southwest of Anchorage.

By the end of 1964, major sewage and water main repairs had been made and some highways were in operation. However, it was estimated that full economic recovery would take four years.

In spite of such difficulties, Alaska began to prepare for the hundredth anniversary of United States purchase. The gala celebration, planned by a Centennial commission, included a program of typical Alaskan activities, such as Eskimo games, sled-dog races, Indian dances, blanket tosses, Eskimo dances, and whale hunts. There were music festivals, ski tournaments, historic pageants recreating events of the past, parades, street dancing, and riverboat races.

ALASKA TODAY

In Alaska today the world can witness the spectacle of "America growing from a rugged frontier to a great new land before its very eyes." However, as someone has slyly remarked, "It is, however, a very comfortable frontier." Here log cabins may still be found nestling almost within the shadow of skyscrapers.

This new frontier has been "discovered" four times within the past century: at the time of its purchase, during the gold rushes, in World War II, and, finally, at the time of statehood. It has been called a "dynamic, spirited, restless, changing, imaginative society." This spirit is probably aided by the fact that there are so many young people there.

People of all races and pursuits have been brought together—the bush pilot, Eskimo seal hunter, Indian fisherman, prospector, big-game guide, serviceman, businessman, housewife, oil man, pipeline worker—in a society where few recognize either caste or class.

In the ten years between the census of 1950 and that of 1960, the population of Alaska gained 75.8 percent. The next decade brought only a 33 percent increase. The native populations have begun to increase and flourish. The 1970 census found a population of over fifty thousand Indians, Aleut, and Eskimo, all to some degree being caught up in the fast-moving new Alaska.

In the 1970s, events of note have included the 1971 Alaskan Native Land Claims Settlement Act, the beginning of the controversial Alaska pipeline in 1974, and the vote of the people of Alaska in 1976 to move the capital city from Juneau to Willow.

In spite of all the progress and development of the last many years, a large percentage of the population still huddles in an area around Anchorage. Much of the state, especially to the north, lies empty except for a few prospectors and Eskimo villages. The real growth and development are still to come. Alaska remains the nation's modern frontier.

One of the aboveground sections of the Trans-Alaska pipeline, which carries oil from the Prudhoe Bay area in the far north to Valdez, in the far south.

Wild flowers, green grass, and green-leaved trees may be seen in Alaska in springtime, even in the Mendenhall Glacier area (above).

Natural Treasures

Everything about Alaska has always been spoken of in superlatives. The legend is told about the airport attendant who pumped 50 gallons (190 liters) of gasoline into what he thought was an airplane before he discovered it was a mosquito. A true story is told of an excited Indian who came to camp calling out that he had been chased by an animal so large it hid the sun. When Europeans in the party went with him to investigate, they found tracks 2 feet (.6 meter) across, spaced 8 feet (2.4 meters) apart.

The maker of the tracks was never found, but the incident brings to mind the huge mastodons and mammoths that roamed Alaska in prehistoric times, as well as smaller animals such as bison, horses, and camels. The most fascinating fact about discovering the remains of such ancient animals in Alaska is that in some areas the perpetual freeze has sometimes preserved the flesh. Since bones are the only remains of these creatures generally found, the preserved flesh is of great value to scientific study. An Alaskan dog once ate, without any ill effects, the fat of a prehistoric animal preserved by the cold for possibly twenty thousand years. The most interesting remains of ancient creatures ever found were the preserved head, trunk, and foreleg of a baby mammoth, now preserved by refrigeration.

CLIMATE

Sequoias found in petrified forests indicate that the climate of Alaska at one time might have been temperate in its now frigid parts.

Today there is no tropical weather in Alaska, but the state has almost every other variation of climate that might be experienced in the other states from Maine through California.

The Panhandle has moderate winters about like those of Maryland, and cool summers. Rain is the predominating feature, with as much as 150 inches (381 centimeters) a year at Ketchikan. Even in the central region as far west as Homer, the grass may be green as early as February.

Southwest Alaska is called the "Weather Kitchen," and much of the weather of all North America is influenced here. Winters in the area are known for their terrible windstorms, with fierce gales up to 90 miles (145 kilometers) per hour.

There are temperature extremes in the interior, with a range of 100 degrees above zero Fahrenheit (37.8 degrees Celsius) to 70 degrees below zero Fahrenheit (-56.7 degrees Celsius). Even Fort Yukon has had 100-degree temperatures, exceeding the maximum ever experienced at Palm Beach, Florida. Fairbanks in winter is known as the land of electric hitching posts, where automobiles instead of horses are tied. These posts on the street use electric warmers to keep car radiators from freezing.

In Fairbanks a car with a seventeen-quart (sixteen-liter) radiator will need twelve quarts (eleven liters) of anti-freeze. A car left standing in one spot too long may have tires that are flattened out by freezing where they touched the ground. And yet, Fairbanks has a growing season of a hundred days. Interior Alaska is the state's driest area, with as little as 7 inches (17.8 centimeters) of moisture a year, but the land is a swamp due to lack of evaporation and permafrost, which halts absorption. The dogs learn to turn aside in cold weather, to avoid the spark of static electricity from a friendly pat.

At Barrow the sea ice breaks up only long enough for ships to bring in the year's supplies. When the sun rises at Barrow, it does not set for ninety-two days. It also fails to come above the horizon for two months in winter. Someone has said that Alaska is the only state where a drive-in movie could have matinees. In winter, the mailman sometimes has to use a flashlight on his rounds.

A PROFUSION OF FLOWERS

In season, Alaska is a paradise of wild flowers. Even in the tundra are found mountain azalea, cushion pink, forget-me-not (state flower), alpine spring beauty, blue lupine, native peas, asters, cinquefoil, larkspur, monkshood, lichens, and moss. The tundra of the forbidding Seward Peninsula, where Nome is located, supports

In season, Alaska is a paradise of wild flowers.

the amazing variety of three hundred different wild flowers. There are thirty varieties of orchids in the state.

In the bleaker portions of the state, many familiar plants are dwarfed or stunted into startling forms by wind or weather. Dwarf dandelions grow to a height of only 1 inch (2.5 centimeters). Willow trees in some areas are as small as clover plants. The tiny creeping dogwood, however, startlingly has 1-inch (2.5-centimeter) flowers— normal size.

In other parts, wild flowers make Alaska a garden. On mountain slopes, Alpine blooms push through the snow at the first touch of warmth. In summer a common and spectacular blossom is the 6-foot-tall (1.8 meters) magenta-colored spike of the fireweed plant.

The Alaskan polar bear (above) grows to be nearly as big as the huge Alaskan brown bears. Caribou (right) thrive in the Alaskan climate.

Most unusual is Alaskan cotton, topped with a wavy ball of cotton-like seeds that give it that name. Another interesting plant is goatsbeard, with creamy plumes 4 feet (1.2 meters) high.

Many mountain slopes are bright with wild flowers. Wild hyacinth, cowslip, bog laurel, violets, arctic daisy, wood nymph, and dramatic butter-yellow skunk cabbage all add to the profusion of color. Cultivated gardens produce spectacular flowers such as 9-foot (2.7-meter) delphiniums. Many prize contests are held for Alaska gardeners, who can coax a dozen varieties of roses to bloom.

The seed pod of the wild rose served the early population of Alaska as a fruit; many other plants were also carefully used. The rice lily, a deep-colored, almost black-blossomed plant, produces a bulb that was boiled and eaten by the Indians. Other edible plants were goose tongue, wild parsley, and cucumber (streptopus).

LAND OF DONNER AND BLITZEN

Caribou were originally found in Alaska but were almost exterminated in certain coastal regions. Then under the leadership of Dr. Sheldon Jackson, 1,280 reindeer were introduced to Alaska from

Siberia during the period from 1892 to 1902. Dr. Jackson hoped this would give the Eskimo a more dependable source of food, sinews for thread, and skins for clothing, sleeping bags, and other necessities.

Dr. Jackson was right. Sheep or cows would have starved on the tundra, but reindeer thrived. About 200,000 square miles (518,000 square kilometers) of Alaska are considered suitable only for reindeer or caribou. The reindeer did so well that commercial interests began to slaughter them for meat, dog food, and hides. Alarmed that the Eskimo might once again be cheated out of their living, Congress, in 1937, passed a bill to retain ownership of reindeer solely for the benefit of the residents. At one time there were more than a million reindeer in Alaska, but today possibly only fifty thousand are left. However, there are now many caribou.

Some members of the deer family grow unusually large in Alaska. Alaska moose are the largest of the deer breed. A snorting, pawing moose sometimes may challenge an Alaska Railroad train and force it to slow down or halt. Bull moose in Alaska weigh as much as three quarters of a ton (.68 metric ton).

Bull moose in Alaska weigh as much as three quarters of a ton.

Alaskan brown bears are now the world's largest bears and the largest land-dwelling meat eaters alive today. The bears of Kodiak Island are probably the largest of all; although they are known as Kodiak bears, they are the same as Alaska browns, a variety of grizzly. These bears, enormously strong, are even able to drag the carcass of a moose. They fight fiercely when cornered but are usually mild-mannered. They love to fish for salmon and have a rollicking time when the fish are running.

Kodiak bears are among the world's most prized hunting trophies, and hunting is carefully regulated.

Alaska has the world's most colorful assortment of bears—black, white (polar), brown, cinnamon, a bluish-colored bear called glacier, and grizzly. The famous Toklat grizzlies of the Alaska Range have been seen rolling back yards of tundra with their huge paws, looking for mice.

The last of Alaska's native musk ox had been killed by 1865, but thirty-four were brought to Fairbanks in 1930 and transferred to Nunivak Island. Bison were imported in 1927. Their increase was phenomenal. Strangely, bison grow much larger in Alaska than they do in the prairie states.

Many valuable fur animals were killed or diminished by intensive hunting. The sea otter was almost gone, and the Alaska fur seal was nearly destroyed. Happily, however, in 1912, the beautiful and interesting seal was brought under strict United States control and saved from extinction in an agreement with Russia and Canada. Hunting is carefully regulated in the Pribilof Island breeding

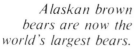

Alaskan brown bears are now the world's largest bears.

Walruses are invaluable to the Eskimo.

grounds, and there are now more than a million and a half of these much-prized animals. Fortunately, too, the sea otter has made a comeback, and there are now about thirty thousand of them in the Aleutians.

Other fur bearers of Alaska include ermine, land otter, wolverine, muskrat, beaver, lynx, marten, mink, and foxes of many colors— red, white, silver, blue, and "cross."

The mighty "whale horse" or *hvalros* (walrus) of the Norwegians is invaluable to the Eskimo. From walrus intestines they make rain-coats and windows. The meat is used for food and the tusks for beautiful carvings. The hide is used for umiak coverings. Whales regularly provide living needs for courageous Eskimo hunters of Point Hope and Barrow.

Alaska's mountains harbor the handsome Dall sheep, mountain goats, and other animals.

Among the smaller animals, the snowshoe hare is one of the most interesting; it sports outsized feet, like snowshoes, for easy snow travel in winter. For protection, it changes its color from white in the snow period to brown in summer. Lemmings are also found in Alaska.

IN SEA AND AIR

Probably fish still would be rated as the most valuable of Nature's treasures in Alaska.

Five kinds of salmon spawn in Alaska water—all of them of great value, with red or sockeye salmon of Bristol Bay the most choice for canning. King salmon brings a high price, but it is not canned. A unique Alaska monster is the giant king crab, sometimes measuring 7 feet (2.1 meters) from claw to claw. The crab industry is centered at Kodiak. Cordova is called the razor-clam capital of the world. Petersburg cocktail shrimp are world famous.

Strangely, marine life is more numerous in Bering Sea waters than in warmer oceans. Apparently, this is because of a greater amount of oxygen. Tiny plankton grow abundantly in colder waters to provide more food. The waters teem with life.

Inland, sport fishermen find the finest fishing, with such choices as salt-water salmon, rainbow trout, steelheads, cutthroats, dolly vardens, grayling, and Arctic char. An amazing fish is the Alaska blackfish, of tundra pools. It can revive after being frozen. When thawed, blackfish return to normal activity. Eskimo fishermen use them for dog food.

The number of birds nesting in Alaska is amazing, although a large percentage of them migrate south for the winter. Even the Arctic Circle contains important bird-nesting grounds. Among the most interesting birds is the surfbird. Twice each year at least some of them fly the enormous distance from central Alaska to the far Pacific coast of South America. They breed in the mountains of Alaska, but are so elusive, such masters of concealment, that their nesting grounds were unknown until 1921. The first nest and eggs were found in 1926 in Mt. McKinley Park.

Other birds arrive from distant lands to spend the summer—the longtailed jaeger from Japan and the golden plover from Hawaii, among others. Alaskan birds vary from the tiny hummingbird of southeastern Alaska to the mighty bald eagles that congregate in large numbers along the Chilkat River in the fall to feed on dead salmon. The concentration of bald eagles on the Chilkat is amazing, some three thousand at one time. Golden eagles, gyrfalcons, and other hawks are also found, as are many owls.

Ptarmigan are the grouse of the tundra and mountain country. Their feathered feet help them to snowshoe over the snow in winter, when their feathers are snow white. There are also many other kinds of grouse, including spruce, sooty, sheep-tailed, and Franklin. Magpie, Canada jay, stellar jay, and chickadee have also adapted themselves to the winter weather. Vast numbers of whistling swans, ducks, geese, and some trumpeter swans breed in Alaska; loons, grebes, gulls, and other waterfowl are common. Songbirds include varied thrush, robin, horned lark, junco, redpoll, white-crowned sparrow, longspur, snow bunting, warblers, and many others.

FORESTS, MINERALS, AND FOAMING WATER

In Alaska, 137 million acres (55.4 million hectares) of land support forests. About 44 million acres (17.8 million hectares) have commercial possibilities. Hemlock makes up about 73 percent, spruce 21 percent, and cedar 5 percent of the commercial forest lands. Tongass National Forest of more than 16 million acres (nearly 6.5 million hectares) is the largest in the United States. Chugach National Forest of nearly 5 million acres (nearly 2 million hectares) is the second largest in the country.

The limits of forest growth are spreading farther north and west. Some extend fifty miles (eighty kilometers) farther than they did a few decades ago, indicating a warming trend of climate.

The federal government rates thirty-three minerals as critical to the nation's needs. Of these, thirty-two are found in Alaska. Much of the mineral wealth of Alaska is still to be surveyed. Just what wonderful finds will come to light cannot even be guessed now, but it is assumed that the state is only at the beginning of its mineral discoveries.

Announcement in late 1964 of one of the largest finds of iron-ore deposits anywhere on the Alaska Peninsula was a signal for worldwide excitement. After the announcement came, it was learned that the geologists of a Standard Oil Company of Indiana subsidiary had been quietly working for months to map and stake their iron claims. Other huge iron-ore deposits near Dillingham, the Klukwan deposits near Haines, and the newly discovered source near Wrangell up the Stikine River are among the known iron-ore resources of the state.

Considerable oil and huge deposits of natural gas in northern Alaska have already been tapped, and Alaskan oil is now helping the United States to battle the energy crisis. The controversial Trans-Alaska pipeline carries oil from the Prudhoe Bay area in the far north to Valdez, 800 miles (1,287 kilometers) to the south. From there, the oil is transported by tankers to refineries in Washington and California. A natural-gas pipeline will be begun soon, probably paralleling the oil pipeline.

Gold is still being taken from Alaska, and many authorities indicate that there probably still are large reserves of gold to be found there. One hunter in Alaska automatically became a prospector when he found a large gold nugget wedged in the cleft hoof of a moose he had shot.

Silver, platinum, antimony, arsenic, chromium, manganese, bismuth, mercury, copper, nickel, molybdenum, lead, zinc, tungsten, asbestos, garnet, sand, gravel, barite, uranium, cobalt, graphite, sulphur, and jade are all known, and probably exist in much larger quantities than ever yet have been discovered. As Alaska grows in population, building stone, gravel-road ballast, sand, clays, limestone, and other non-metallic minerals gain increasing importance.

Coal reserves in Alaska amount to an estimated 100 billion tons (91 billion metric tons), and water power is everywhere. Alaska is thought to have the largest undeveloped water-power resources on the continent.

People Use Their Treasures

WEALTH WITH FINS

Since Alaska was purchased in 1867, the value of its fish harvest has totaled more than three and one-half billion dollars. This is many times the value of all the gold that has come from Alaska in the same period. An annual value of fisheries' products of nearly two hundred million dollars once was Alaska's economic mainstay, but this changed as more and more new enterprises came in and population increased.

Salmon accounts for almost two-fifths of the annual catch, with halibut second. The king crab industry is next in value, with its headquarters at Kodiak. Trout, halibut, grayling, Arctic char, shee fish, herring, cod, and shrimp also have commercial importance. Petersburg is one of the important seafood processing communities, packing millions of pounds in a year's time, principally halibut.

WEALTH WITH NEEDLES

Two billion board feet can be cut from the forests of Alaska every year, and those magnificent resources will continue to reproduce themselves indefinitely. The Tongass National Forest alone can pro-

Commercial fishing, formerly Alaska's economic mainstay, is still important.

duce a sustained yield of more than a billion board feet. Because of its unique location, the Tongass National Forest in southeast Alaska is the only national forest where lumber is transported to mill and to market entirely by sea. Chugach National Forest, in the central coast region, ranks as the next most important lumber source of the state.

Alaska's state tree, the Sitka spruce, is one of the valuable commercial trees in Alaska.

Lumber, and the industries based on lumber, promise to be the largest business of Alaska in the future. In 1956 a $52 million pulp mill opened at Ketchikan. This marked the beginning of a great new industry for the state. This mill and the one at Sitka, opened in 1960, bring in a large part of the state's ''export'' dollars. Substantial pulp-mill expansion is expected with the development of hydroelectric power in the area.

Much of the pulp is destined for the rayon and paper industries of Japan. Japanese capital has helped to finance the pulp-mill expansion of Alaska. Japanese industrialists are taking increasing interest in the cooperation between their country, which lacks natural resources but has great manufacturers, and Alaska, which has enormous resources but little manufacturing. Alaska-Japan trade is expected to expand rapidly.

MINERAL WEALTH

The wealth of gold first put Alaska on the map. In the years since the Alaska purchase, over a billion dollars in gold has enriched the coffers of the country—more than a hundred times the original purchase price. Although gold mining has declined today, gold in total value worth more than the purchase price still comes from Alaska each year.

At one time the Alaska-Juneau Company carried on the largest gold-mining operation in the world in terms of number of tons of ore processed. However, this was also the lowest-grade gold ore in the world mined at a profit. The mine, with its shafts running upward, not down, was closed in 1944.

Gold-mining methods have changed fantastically since the first prospectors came in. Today the modern pan dredges of such firms as U.S. Smelting and Refining Company can process 15,000 tons (13,600 metric tons) of ore-bearing soils a day. When necessary, water is brought many miles down the hills in flumes to wash the gold from the gravel. In some years the mining companies in Alaska have moved almost as much dirt as was moved in building the Panama Canal.

Oil is the mineral causing most excitement in Alaska today. Because many geologists list Alaska as one of the country's major oil-bearing regions, every major oil company in the world is prospecting there. This is a rugged, costly business. For example, north of the Brooks Range, oil-drilling exploration can be done only in the severe winter weather. In summer the thawed surface will not support drilling rigs.

On the Kenai Peninsula, the first commercial well in Alaska began to produce 900 barrels (123 metric tons) of crude oil per day in 1957. This was Alaska's first major oil field. A ten-million-dollar Standard Oil refinery was opened there in 1963 to process the field's output. Development of offshore oil in Cook Inlet was begun in 1964.

Alaskan petroleum production in 1961 was only 6 million barrels (nearly 820 thousand metric tons). At peak production, Alaska oil is expected to approach 1 million barrels per day (136 thousand metric tons).

During World War I, copper mining in Alaska exceeded the value of gold. In the period between 1911 and 1938 the great Kennecott Copper Mine at the mouth of the Copper River at Cordova produced 100 million dollars worth of copper and employed six hundred miners in 40 miles (64 kilometers) of underground tunnels, until the ore ran out and the mill was shut down. At present, copper is not one of the state's leading minerals, but some expect that it may be again some day, due to the huge deposits being developed on the Kobuk River by the Kennecott Company.

Since the purchase, more than 4 billion dollars in mineral wealth has come from Alaska. About 400 million dollars per year is the current valuation.

Because of the many hours of summer sunshine, most of the vegetables and berries grown in Alaska are at least double the average size. Cabbages as large as those pictured above are fairly common. Below: A fertile farm at Dillingham.

WEALTH FROM THE SOIL

About 1,000,000 acres (400,000 hectares) in Alaska are now suitable for farming, and to date less than 30,000 acres (12,000 hectares) have been put into production. The state could produce 50 percent of its food needs, but currently is producing only about 10 percent. Consequently, most provisions are shipped in from outside, increasing the cost of living. Large quantities of fresh fruits and vegetables are flown in every day.

More than half of the farming of Alaska is concentrated around the Alaska Railroad. Matanuska Valley produces nearly three-fourths of the state's crops. This former wilderness has become a distinctively American community. Tanana Valley is another currently productive region, and there are many other rich valleys still waiting for development.

The many hours of summer sunshine result in extraordinary yields. Most of the vegetables and berries grown in Alaska are at least double the average size. Strawberries are enormous. Sometimes one strawberry, sliced, is said to be enough for a serving, although this may be a slight Alaskan exaggeration. The size of cabbage heads is unbelievable. (The record is 61 pounds or 28 kilograms.) Potatoes, lettuce, carrots, radishes, celery, barley, and oats all flourish.

TRANSPORTATION AND COMMUNICATION

"The flyingest people in the world!"—Alaskans have that title because the vast distances and comparative lack of roads make flying a necessity. Seventy-eight percent of the population uses air transportation regularly. Flying has reshaped Alaskan life. The family "car" in Alaska is often a pontoon plane, parked on a nearby lake. Everyone flies—"doctors to patients, women to hairdressers, lawmakers to the legislature." One eighteen-year-old Indian girl flew her own plane 600 miles (966 kilometers) to register at the University of Alaska.

Because of the vast distances and comparative lack of roads, flying is a necessity in Alaska. The family "car" is often an amphibian plane.

Lake Hood, near Anchorage, is almost filled with private planes of residents, many of whom commute to vacation lakeside homes in their seaplanes. There are so many private planes that a helicopter tow-truck service has been established.

Commercial aviation has turned to Alaska, for it has become the "crossroads of the world." Busy Anchorage International Airport is one of the country's major air centers. Many flights stop over there on their way to remote parts of the world, on the great-circle flight routes. The northernmost major airport on the continent is at Fairbanks.

More than eight hundred Alaska communities have scheduled air service. Where there are no commercial routes, experienced bush pilots can put down on frozen lakes, winding rivers, even mud flats or gravel bars.

Despite the wide use of airplanes, one of Alaska's greatest needs is an increase in highway and railroad mileage. The first railroad in Alaska was opened on July 29, 1900. It was finished in only two years, with materials rushed 2,000 miles (3,200 kilometers) for the job. This was the narrow-gauge White Pass and Yukon railroad route of gold-rush fame. Experts had said that this was a railroad that could never be built, but courage, skill, and determination did the job.

Owned and operated by the United States government, the 470-mile (756-kilometer) mainline and 67 miles (108 kilometers) of branch line of the Alaska Railroad stretch from Seward and Whittier north through Anchorage to Fairbanks. Only two United States railroads are government owned, this and one in the Panama Canal

Zone. Alaska trainmen are friendly people. They make special stops for sportsmen and carry messages to isolated prospectors and homesteaders.

One of the most unusual railroads anywhere was the one built from Nome to Anvil Creek in 1901. It was called the Wild Goose Railroad. During the summer thaws, the tracks sank into the ground, and no one knew quite where to find them. In spite of this problem, it paid for its cost in the first year of operation.

Water routes were Alaska's first means of transportation, and still remain most important for freight. They say that the first ship built on the western shores of America was launched in Resurrection Bay in 1794. At one time Sitka was the busiest port of the entire west coast of North America. The first steamboat chugged up the mighty Yukon at the astonishingly early date of 1866. This river is navigable for 1,700 miles (2,736 kilometers) during the open season and has been called the superhighway of early Alaska, busy with barges and stern wheelers. The major portion of its navigable length, 1,265 miles (2,036 kilometers), is in Alaska.

In 1963, the state of Alaska opened a new marine highway by providing a unique state ferry service. In the southeastern section, ferries operate between Prince Rupert, British Columbia, and Skagway, Alaska, serving Ketchikan, Wrangell, Petersburg, Sitka, Juneau, and Haines on the way and carrying passengers and automobiles. Another state ferry operates on a route covering Seward, Kodiak, Homer, and Anchorage. A third ferry system serves between Valdez and Cordova.

Alaska provides a unique state ferry service.
This is the ferry at Tea Harbor, near Juneau.

The first highway in Alaska was made passable to horse sleds in 1907 by General W.P. Richardson. It was known then as the Richardson Trail. In 1910 it was improved for use by wagons from Valdez to Fairbanks. In the days before the automobile, the trip required eight days. In 1913 one automobile made the trip. Now the Richardson Highway connects Valdez with the Alaska Highway.

The Alaska Highway, built during World War II, has given many an adventurous motorist a new travel experience over its 1,523 miles (2,451 kilometers) from Dawson Creek, British Columbia, to Fairbanks. (The stretch of road from Big Delta Junction to Fairbanks is actually the Richardson Highway.) Motorists who use the state ferry can connect with the Alaska Highway on the Haines cutoff road. The Denali Highway opens Mt. McKinley National Park to automobile traffic.

There are now over 10,000 miles (16,093 kilometers) of streets and highways in Alaska. The village of Circle in the Yukon is the most northerly point in the state reached by road.

The part played by dogsled in Alaska transportation can scarcely be exaggerated in both utility and romance. The dogs made an especially valuable contribution to the carrying of mail. However, the days of dogsled transportion are largely over in present-day Alaska, except for use by the Eskimo.

The first newspaper published in Alaska was the *Esquimeaux,* created for members of the Western Union exploration of 1866. The first commercial newspaper was the Alaska *Times,* put out by a Sitka tailor in 1868. The *Nome Nugget,* founded in 1899, is the oldest Alaska newspaper in continuing circulation. The *Daily News-Miner* of Fairbanks is America's northernmost daily newspaper. Cable connections between Alaska and the rest of the United were completed in 1903.

When radio first came to Anchorage, station KFQD was so popular that Eskimo mothers named their sons for its announcers. Radio continues to have a particularly important place in bringing weather and other news across the vast reaches of the state. The United States Public Health Service gives medical advice over the air and arranges to have urgent cases flown in for medical attention.

Human Treasures

IN EARLY TIMES

Vitus Bering, the Danish navigator who led Russian exploring parties, and who was the discoverer of Alaska, may be one of the most underrated of the great explorers. Before he could even begin his real explorations, he had to overcome incredible difficulties. In order to get to the Pacific Coast of Asia, Bering and his party had to push from the populated section of Russia through the unexplored frozen wastes of Siberia. They fought their slow way through three devastating winters.

Bering's group dragged an extraordinary quantity of supplies across 2,000 miles (3,219 kilometers) of wilderness. Included in these supplies were the anchors, rigging, cable, and other fittings needed to build a ship when they reached the Pacific. Ten years of subsequent exploration in the *Gabriel* brought Bering near, but not to, American land.

At last, in 1741, an expedition of Bering's came in sight of the peak he named Mt. St. Elias, in southeastern Alaska. They went ashore at what is known as Kayak Island, where they found a timber house of the Indians and took several articles of supplies. Bering insisted on leaving a pound (.5 kilogram) of tobacco, a piece of silk, a Chinese pipe, and an iron kettle in payment for the articles the group had taken.

Bering died on the return voyage, as did many of his men, and he was buried on the lonely island that now bears his name.

For nineteen years, from 1799 to 1818, a Siberian drygoods salesman, Alexander Baranof, was master of all Alaska. He has been described as a "man of iron will, shrewd, competent." As chief director of the Russian-American Company, his word was law. He was feared but respected. In addition to his other talents, Baranof was a poet and song writer. A revealing note which he wrote about his life in Alaska reads in part: "Though Nature is wild here, and the nations bloodthirsty, we endure our sorrows and toil—for profits are important, the motherland needs them . . . We are not after rank or riches, but agreeable brotherhood. Yet what we have earned through striving and toil our descendants will give thanks for!"

In the early days at Sitka, there was toil and suffering. The colony would have died of starvation without the aid of grain from far-off California.

Like so many of the other early Russian colonizers and explorers, Baranof, too, died on the long voyage back to the motherland, of which he spoke so highly. He was seventy-two years old.

MEN OF GOD

The first religious teacher of Alaska was Father Ivan Veniaminov, who worked for ten years among the Aleut peoples at Unalaska. William Dall described Father Veniaminov as a man who "dealt justly and loved mercy ... He learned their language, studied with affectionate comprehension their manners and customs, recorded the climatic and physical conditions under which they lived. . . . " He managed the remarkable task of translating parts of the Bible and several prayers and hymns into the Aleut language.

Later he was sent to Sitka. Among other unusual tasks, he is said to have constructed the tower clock of St. Michael's Cathedral with his own hands. In 1841 Father Veniaminov became the first Bishop (Bishop Innokenti) of Alaska and later had the title Innokenti, Metropolitan of Moscow and Koloma. He died in Russia in 1879.

Among the remarkable men of Alaska history, and among those who have made the greatest contributions to Alaskan welfare, is the Reverend Dr. Sheldon Jackson. He came to Alaska as a missionary and later was named general agent for education in Alaska. In this post he proved remarkably effective in turning the interest of Congress toward Alaska and influencing legislation favorable to the region.

In 1890, Dr. Jackson made an extensive tour of Eskimo settlements to lay plans for educational work. He saw that the Alaskan Eskimo would soon be almost without game, and yet only fifty miles (eighty kilometers) away, in Siberia, the Asians were flourishing.

They had learned to semi-domesticate the caribou, and their large herds of reindeer provided for most of their needs.

When Dr. Jackson failed to interest Congress in plans to bring reindeer to Alaska, he raised $2,136 by contribution and brought in 16 deer in 1891 and 171 in 1892. Congress then made an appropriation for more deer. The Alaskan Eskimo knew nothing of keeping tame reindeer. Herders from Lapland were brought in to teach them. A young Eskimo would agree to an apprenticeship of several years in reindeer husbandry. At the end of his first year he was given six breeding deer, then eight, then ten more. At the end of his apprenticeship he became a herder on his own, and in turn hired apprentices. Within a generation, this unique system rescued the Eskimo from threat of extinction and put them on the road to comparative wealth.

For this one contribution alone, Dr. Jackon deserves to be ranked with our most imaginative thinkers. However, he became involved in political controversy in Alaska, and in 1906 President Theodore Roosevelt removed him from office. (At least one source says he resigned.) But by this time Dr. Sheldon Jackson had become one of the best-loved figures of America, and his reputation remains secure.

MEN OF SCIENCE

America's great naturalist and foremost conservationist, John Muir, came to Alaska in 1879. The next year, with his dog, Stickeen, he explored the great glacier that bears his name. "I had frequently to cross ice bridges that were only knife edges for twenty or thirty feet," Muir wrote, "cutting off the sharp tops and leaving them flat so little Stickeen could follow me."

At one place Muir was almost trapped but decided to try to cross. "When I was doing this, Stickeen came up behind me, pushed his head over my shoulder, looked into the crevasses . . . and looked in my face muttering and whining as if to say, 'Surely you are not going down there.' "

*Dall sheep (above)
were named for
Dr. W.H. Dall,
who explored in Alaska.*

Muir cut a hazardous path across and made it to the other side. "All this dreadful time poor little Stickeen was crying as if his heart was broken ... as if trying to say that he never, never could get down there. ... Finally in despair he hushed his cries, slid his little feet slowly into my footsteps out on the sliver as if holding his breath, while the snow was falling, and the wind was moaning and threatening to blow him off.... He looked up along the row of notched steps I had made, as if fixing them in his mind, then with a nervous spring he whizzed up and passed me on the level ice and ran and cried and barked and rolled about, fairly hysterical in triumphant joy."

Dr. W.H. Dall, for whom the Dall sheep were named, also did much exploring in Alaska. Dall sheep are somewhat similar to the bighorns of the Rocky Mountains.

Father Bernard Hubbard came to be known as the "Glacier Priest" because of his studies of volcanoes and glaciers in Austria. Later, Father Hubbard came from California and traveled extensively in Alaska, writing many scientific papers and such books as *Mush, You Malemutes* and *Cradle of the Storm*.

SUCH INTERESTING PEOPLE

Harriet Pullen, known affectionately as Mother Pullen, arrived at Skagway at the same time as the early Klondike prospectors, "a widow with a brood of little boys clinging to her skirts, and seven dollars in her pockets." During the day she drove a heavy freight wagon with four horses over the awful passes near Skagway.

At night, using a small oven in a tent, she baked pies from dried apples. These sold for "fabulous sums" to hungry men, who found very little other good food in the area. Mother Pullen made her baking pans from discarded tin cans, hammering them into shape. She cut the tops from beer bottles and ground the rough edges away in the sand to make drinking glasses.

In appreciation for her nursing, a local Indian chief gave her a ceremonial robe of ermine trimmed in fine beadwork. She became a blood sister of many tribes and spoke several Indian dialects. Mother Pullen prospered and finally was able to build and operate a fine hotel, the Pullen House, at Skagway. It had modern conveniences and banquet halls. Food was served on Haviland china and a solid silver service designed by the skilled owner herself. Just across the bay, she owned and managed a ranch and a fine dairy farm. In her hotel she collected curios of the early days—copper and silver candlesticks of the Russian days, rare trade beads, and many Indian relics.

One of Mother Pullen's sons, Daniel D., was the first Alaska boy to be accepted at West Point; he became a football hero there, and during World War I won the Distinguished Service Cross. His brother, Captain Royal Pullen, also distinguished himself during the war, so that General Pershing said, "I wish I had a regiment of Pullens!" This was a fine tribute to the family of a pioneer mother who should be remembered as one of the remarkable women of America.

At the opposite extreme, Jefferson Smith was "one of the world's truly notorious bad men." He gained the nickname "Soapy Smith" by wrapping five-dollar bills around cakes of soap and selling them for a dollar each. Of course, he palmed each five dollar bill before the buyer got his soap.

Soapy Smith and his gang terrorized Skagway, murdering and robbing and fleecing people with confidence games and crooked gambling. Soapy looked like a fine gentleman and gave liberally to his church in Skagway, although his followers sometimes broke into the church and took the contributions back. Finally, a large group of townspeople met on the wharf to decide what could be done about Soapy. They posted Frank Reid as guard. Hearing of the meeting, Soapy Smith hurried down alone. Both he and Reid drew and fired at the same instant, and the terror of Skagway was no more. Unfortunately, the town's liberator also was killed. On his lonely tombstone was carved the inscription, "Frank H. Reid, Died July 20, 1898. He gave his life for the honor of Skagway.

The artistic character of the Eskimo people is evident in the work of several prominent Eskimo artists, including Howard Rock (Skivoan Weyahok), sculptor and painter of Arctic subjects, and George Aden Ahgupuk (Twok), noted for his line drawings made on bleached reindeer hide.

Sidney Laurence is called the dean of Alaska's artists. His painting of Mt. McKinley is displayed in the Smithsonian Institution at Washington, D.C.

Prominent writers associated with Alaska include Rex Beach and Jack London. In *The Iron Trail*, Rex Beach immortalized the Copper River Northwestern Railroad. For a time Beach lived at Stevens Village, and he used the town as the background for *The Barrier*. Beach's book *The Spoilers,* gives a vivid picture of the early days of Nome.

Jack London (right), excited by tales of gold, went to the Yukon in 1897, when he was twenty-one years old. He was disappointed in his search for gold, but during the short year he spent there, he stored up a wealth of material for later books and short stories.

Teaching and Learning

Alaskan education began with the founder of Russian colonies in America, Gregory Shelikov. He and his wife taught the people of Kodiak beginning in 1784. The first school in Sitka was begun in 1805, and in 1820 a school for navigation and trades was opened.

The great early educational effort in Alaska was made by American missionaries—Presbyterian in the southeast; Moravian at Kuskokwim and upper Bristol Bay; Roman Catholic at Holy Cross; Methodist in the Alaska Peninsula and Aleutians; Baptist at Cook Inlet and Prince William Sound; Episcopalian in the difficult interior and to the north; and Congregationalist along the Bering Sea and Strait. There were Swedish and Norwegian missions on Norton Sound and Port Clarence.

Today, Alaska has a modern system of public education, recruiting the finest teachers from other states, as well as those trained locally. Evidence of the importance Alaskans place on education is the large percentage of the state's total budget that is invested in educational work. This may be one of the reasons why students rank well above the national average in grades, I.Q., and work accomplished. There are few dropouts. Even in weather that reaches forty degrees below zero (Fahrenheit and Celsius), Eskimo children think nothing of walking miles for tutoring.

In 1922 six men entered the first class of the Alaska Agricultural College and School of Mines, a United States land-grant college—the first college in Alaska. Today that institution is the University of Alaska, a modern university that is the northernmost in the world.

The work of its Geophysical Institute is world renowned, and its School of Mines is recognized as being among the finest of its type. The university's Agricultural Experiment Station has made notable advances in the never-ending search to find new plants and adapt old ones that are suitable for Alaska's climate. The university operates community college branches at Anchorage, Ketchikan, Juneau, Sitka, Palmer, and Kenai.

Alaska Methodist University and the University of Alaska are the only four-year, degree-granting institutions in the state.

Enchantment of Alaska

Visitors in Alaska may travel by ocean liner, automobile, railroad, airplane, dogsled, reindeer sled, or snowmobile. They may eat sourdough hotcakes, Arctic shee fish, or reindeer steaks, as well as typical American dishes. They may pan gold, explore a dormant volcano, clamber over a glacier, experience some of the world's finest skiing, learn about several fascinating cultures, or just view the scenery, which is unsurpassed.

SOUTHEAST: PASSAGE TO PARADISE

Those who visit southeast Alaska are most likely to come on the Alaska State Ferry over the Inside Passage—that spectacular thousand-mile (sixteen-hundred kilometers) marine highway. Here is a land of fiords, where sheer rock walls loom up as much as 2,400 feet (732 meters) from the ocean. In this land of sparkling streams and waterfalls, mountain goats leap from crag to crag and, below them, seals and sea lions sport in the water.

The southernmost Alaska port is Ketchikan, the thriving "Salmon Capital of the World," where tides climb twenty feet (six meters) and where temperatures rarely drop to freezing. With its "back to the wall," Ketchikan's houses, reached by flights of steps, cling tier on tier to the hillside. Here, at Saxman Park, is one of the largest collections of authentic Indian totem poles in the world.

In the vicinity, a number of Haida, Tlingit, and Tsimshian Indians still reside. The principal Haida home is Hydaburg, Prince of Wales Island. The old village of Kasaan was made a national monument by Woodrow Wilson in 1916, but it has since been abandoned. Row upon row of tall totem carvings still may be seen at the Tlingit village of Klawock.

Wrangell received its name in honor of Baron von Wrangell. At Garnet Ledge, near Wrangell, visitors may scratch for their own gar-

Opposite: One of the famous Ketchikan totem poles.

nets. The trip up the Stikine River by boat is considered one of the most spectacular anywhere. With its large Scandinavian population, attracted originally by the commercial fishing, Petersburg is known as Alaska's "Little Norway."

Historic Sitka, on Baranof Island, has preserved a fascinating array of early-day reminders. The Cathedral of St. Michael, built in 1848-1850 and reconstructed after a fire in 1966, is still the spiritual center of the Russion Orthodox faith in Alaska. It is noted for its world-famed collection of religious art.

Sitka National Monument, established in 1910 on the site of the fierce Russian-Indian battles, has one of the finest exhibits of totem poles. Here are the eighteen historic Haida totems once exhibited at the St. Louis World's Fair in 1904. The fifty-nine-foot (eighteen-meter) Fog Woman totem has more carved figures than any other. Skilled totem carvers still may be seen at work; their art is priced by the foot.

At Sitka, on Castle Hill, where the castle burned in 1894, the ceremony of lowering the Imperial Russian flag is reenacted each year to commemorate Alaska's purchase. The old Russian cemetery has headstones dating back to 1804. Also at Sitka is the Alaska Pioneer Home, for elderly Alaskans.

Sheldon Jackson Junior College at Sitka is famous for its museum displays from Russian, Tlingit, Haida, and Eskimo cultures.

"Most scenic capital on the North American Continent" and "The American vale of Kashmir" are just two of many vivid descriptions of Juneau, Alaska's capital city until the move to Willow. Here, on one side, Mt. Juneau crowds its namesake city to the sea. That sea is kept in check by an eighty-foot-high (twenty-four meters) breakwater built with rocks from the Alaska Juneau Mine.

The six-story capitol building was finished in 1930 and was formerly the Federal and Territorial Building. The Alaska Historical Library and Museum has the finest collection of Alaskana anywhere, and the museum has the most complete Eskimo collection in the United States. Visitors are intrigued by such items as fawn-skin baby diapers, with disposable linings of moss, and Eskimo art two thousand years old. Juneau's annual Salmon Derby closes almost every

Left: The Governor's Mansion, Juneau. Below: Alaska's capital city until the move to Willow, Juneau is built at the edge of the sea. Mt. Juneau rises in the background.

shop and activity in the city as ardent fishermen compete for such prizes as automobiles, boats, or tickets to the Rose Bowl game or to Hawaii.

Twelve miles (nineteen kilometers) northwest of Juneau is Mendenhall Glacier, one of the most photographed sights in Alaska. There is an observatory there.

Skagway, during tourist season, stages a rip-roaring "Days of '98" melodrama. This marks the time when the town had a population of twenty thousand instead of its present seven hundred. Relics of those days are preserved in the Trail of '98 Museum. In Gold Rush Cemetery are the graves of Frank Reid and Soapy Smith.

Indian arts and crafts have been revived at Port Chilkoot, where authentic Chilkat dancers also may be seen. Arts and crafts of the Tlingit Indians are preserved in Totem Village at old Fort William H. Seward at Haines (renamed Port Chilkoot).

A showplace of the Western Hemisphere, Glacier Bay was made a national monument in 1925. Over twenty enormous glaciers terminate at or near the bay, in a region of fantastic natural beauty, where whales may spout in the bay and hair seals sleep peacefully on floating cakes of ice.

THE CENTRAL COAST

Anchorage has been called the "Miracle City of Alaska," and its continuing restoration, after the 1964 earthquake disaster, required renewed miracles on the part of everyone. Each February, Anchorage becomes a carnival city with its annual Fur Rendezvous. This recalls the gatherings of the trappers to sell furs, and features a fur auction as well as a miners' and trappers' ball, Eskimo dance, world-championship sled-dog races, and other exciting events. Another reminder of the pioneer past is the trapper's cabin, brought to add interest to the City Hall lawn.

Opposite: Mendenhall Glacier from Auke Lake.

Modern Anchorage has recovered from the 1964 earthquake. Right: Whale sculpture at the Carr-Gotstein Building.

Left: Signpost in Anchorage ("Air Crossroads of the World") shows air miles to some of the great cities of the world.

Although it is Alaska's largest city, Anchorage's golf course still gives the right-of-way to moose and bear, and the wonders of nature are within easy reach. Some of these are displayed in the Jonas Brothers Wildlife Museum there.

Nearby Palmer is the trading center for Matanuska Valley. In the valley, more than five thousand people now make their homes where the original two hundred families came to try their luck.

The Valdez region has been called "The Switzerland of Alaska." Along with Seward and Whittier, this is the northernmost ice-free port on the continent. Nearby Bridal Veil and Horseshoe Falls are showplaces, and the Chitina Valley may someday be one of the world's great recreation areas.

Seward, much damaged in the 1964 earthquake, is known for its mild climate. It was named in honor of Secretary of State William H. Seward, who bought Alaska for the United States. The annual Mount Marathon Race, which includes the climbing of that mountain, is an interesting event.

Seldovia presents an atmosphere of old Russia for the visitor, and Kenai is the fast-growing oil capital of Alaska.

CENTRAL: THE GOLDEN HEART AND LOFTY HEAD

Alaska's third-largest city, Fairbanks, was named for Charles W. Fairbanks, an Indiana senator who later became vice president of the United States under Theodore Roosevelt. It is one of the most extraordinary cities of the United States. In the summer it is the land of the midnight sun, where one of the favorite attractions is the annual midnight-sun baseball game. This begins at 10:30 P.M. and continues through midnight without artificial light.

In winter, Fairbanks must keep antifreeze circulating in its hydrants. To guard against freezing, it was necessary to have the city's water system especially designed. The water in each house circulates through the pipes continuously to keep the water flowing.

Fairbanks calls itself the "Golden Heart of Alaska," and the Golden Days Festival annually celebrates gold-rush days. World championship river-boat races are held at Fairbanks, and the American Sled Dog Championship offers a total of $15,000 in prizes. At suburban College is the University of Alaska, with a fine museum featuring ethnographic, archeological, and historical collections and fine exhibits of Alaska animals and birds. Fifty miles (eighty kilometers) northwest of Fairbanks is the popular health resort of Chena Hot Springs.

South and west of Fairbanks is Nenana, renowed for its ice sweepstakes. Alaskans bet on the exact day, hour, and minute that the ice on the Tanana River will break up and move downstream. Thousands of dollars change hands during this event.

In 1896, W.A. Dickey discovered an immensely high and rugged mountain, which he named McKinley in honor of the president. The Indians called it "Denali." Two prospectors, Taylor and Anderson, climbed the north peak in 1910. In 1913 the Episcopal Archdeacon of the Yukon, Hudson Stuck, headed the first party ever to climb the true summit of Mt. McKinley. In 1917 this 3,000-square-mile (7,800 square kilometers) wildlife wilderness was made a national park. This highland empire, much larger and more majestic than all of Switzerland, is the home of the white Dall sheep.

Not until 1947 did the first woman, Mrs. Bradford Washburn, win her way to the summit. The base is now reached by road and railroad, and there is an airfield.

SOUTHWEST: MOUNTAINS THAT WENT TO SEA

The one-time fury of Mt. Katmai has now passed, at least for the time being. In its blasted summit, a jade-green lake that never freezes is the only evidence of the fires still below. The glacier in the crater of Mt. Katmai is the only one in the world of which an almost exact age is known, since it was born after the eruption in 1912. The region is now Katmai National Monument, at 2,697,590 acres (1,091,677 hectares) the largest of all our national preserves.

On nearby Kodiak Island, the sunshine isle of the Pacific, is Kodiak, the oldest town in Alaska, where the first church in Alaska was built in 1794. Chirikof Island, once a Czarist prison, is now leased by a cattle company. Cowboys ride the range here to supply a part of Alaska's beef.

Adak is the site of the great naval base. As the Aleutian Islands sweep out to sea, they finally reach a point at Attu where they are almost closer to the capital of Japan than that of Alaska.

WEST AND NORTH

Each year, on the lonely Pribilof Islands in the Bering Sea, the annual roundup of fur seals by government herders takes place. At this time the allotted quota is harvested by official fur hunters.

On the same bleak Bering Sea to the north lies Nome. The name Nome was a draftsman's error. On a map, a nearby cape was shown with the words "cape (name?)." Someone overlooked the question mark and thought the word was Nome and the name Cape Nome was born. Nome took its name from Cape Nome. Much of Nome is perpetually askew because the permafrost causes buildings to turn and twist as the ground alternately thaws and freezes. Public buildings in the permafrost area are kept stable by refrigerating their foundations permanently. It is said that if the problem of permafrost could be solved, the result would be as electrifying as turning a desert into a flowering valley.

The ivory carvers of King Island and Little Diomede travel the long distance to Nome each spring by skin boat to sell and barter their beautiful handwork. Eskimo handicraft is said to serve as their "cash crops."

Nome is the scene of the All Alaska Championship Dog Race, a thrilling contest for men, sleds, and teams over the 158-mile (254.3-kilometer) route from Nome to Golovin and back. The Farthest North Bench Show for Malemute and Siberian dogs is also held there.

Kotzebue is probably the largest Eskimo village in the world. Here reindeer meat and the laundry may be seen drying side by side on an Eskimo rack. The Kotzebue Fourth of July festivities are renowned.

Sled dogs at Kotzebue, probably the largest Eskimo village in the world.

Blanket tossers throw the experts high in the air for their daring twists and turns. There is a kayak race and a Miss Arctic Circle contest. In this, the contestants appear smothered in parkas rather than in bathing suits. In this region, the lack of wood requires that whalebone be used as a substitute. One example can be seen in the neat whale-rib picket fence around the Point Hope cemetery.

Far across the state, almost on the Arctic Circle, is Fort Yukon, the oldest English-speaking settlement in Alaska.

From Fort Yukon an unbroken stretch of wilderness must be crossed to reach Barrow, the most northerly town in America. The Arctic Circle (66° 30' north latitude) must also be crossed to reach Barrow. Those who cross the Arctic Circle by air are given a certificate to attest to this fact.

Barrow is the trading center for the whole Arctic coast. To store their food, the people use underground ice caves, which are likely to be full of meat, blubber, and other delicacies. The United States maintains an Arctic Research Laboratory at Barrow.

Nearby is Point Barrow, the jumping-off place. Here hunters still paddle their kayaks and umiaks to hunt walrus, whale, and polar bear. Near here is the memorial to Will Rogers and Wiley Post, who gave the region international prominence in 1935 by their untimely deaths in that bleak world of auroras and midnight sun.

Handy Reference Section

Instant Facts

Became the 49th state, January 3, 1959
Capital—Juneau (in transition)—to be located at Willow
State motto—*North to the Future*
State nickname—*The Great Land* or *The Last Frontier*
State bird—Willow ptarmigan
State fish—King salmon
State flower—Forget-me-not
State tree—Sitka spruce
State gem—Jade
State song—"Alaska's Flag," (music, Elinor Dusenbury; text, Marie Drake)
Area—586,400 square miles (1,518,770 square kilometers)
Rank in area—First
Greatest length (north to south)—800 miles (1,287 kilometers), not including Aleutian and Alexander Archipelagos
Greatest width (east to west)—900 miles (1,448 kilometers), not including Aleutian and Alexander Archipelagos
Geographic center—60 miles (96 kilometers) northwest of Mt. McKinley
Highest point—20,320 feet (6,193 meters), Mt. McKinley
Lowest point—Sea level
Population—352,000 (1975 estimate)
Population density—1.67 persons per square mile (4.3 persons per square kilometer), 1975 estimate
Center of population—33 miles (53 kilometers) southeast of Anchorage

Principal cities—

City	Population (1970 census)
Anchorage	48,061
Spenard (Anchorage suburb)	18,089
Fairbanks	14,771
Fort Richardson	10,751
Fort Wainwright	9,097
Ketchikan	6,994
Juneau	6,050

You Have a Date with History

1728—Vitus Bering discovers Bering Strait
1732—Michael Gvozdev may have touched mainland
1741—First recorded European contact with Alaska mainland, by Bering
1784—First permanent European settlement founded by Russians on Kodiak Island
1799—Old Sitka founded by Alexander Baranof
1799—The Russian-American Company establishes a fur-trade agreement with Russia

1818—Baranof deposed, dies on return voyage to Russia
1867—Alaska purchased by America; Russian-American Company sells business
       to H.M. Hutchinson (Alaska Commercial Co.)
1880—Gold seekers found Juneau
1897—Klondike gold rush populates Skagway
1899—Nome gold rush
1903—Gold discovered at Fairbanks
1912—Alaska established as a U.S. territory; Mt. Katmai explodes
1923—Alaska Railroad completed
1935—Will Rogers, Wiley Post killed at Point Barrow
1942—Attu, Kiska, and Agattu Islands occupied by Japanese
1959—Alaska becomes the 49th state
1964—Disastrous earthquake in south-central Alaska
1968—Large oil reserves discovered near Prudhoe Bay
1974—Alaska pipeline construction begins
1976—Voters approve move of capital to Willow

Government of Alaska Since U.S. Accession

1867-1877 under military occupation.
Made a customs collection district 1877-1879 when it was under rule of the
    customs collector.
1879-1884 under rule of Navy Department.
Organic Act of 1884 provided for civil government and constituted Alaska a civil
    and judicial district. It provided for appointment by the president of the United
    States of a governor of Alaska. Alaska was made a district.
The Criminal Code of 1899 supplemented the Organic Act as did the Civil Code of
    1900 (the Carter Act).
Congress in 1906 passed the Alaska Delegate Bill by which the right to elect one
    delegate to Congress was secured.
From 1906-1912 a territorial form of government was worked on. In 1912
    Congress enacted the Second Organic Act which provided for a Territorial
    Legislature in the Territory of Alaska.
On January 3, 1959 Alaska became the 49th state.

Governors

William Egan, 1958-1966
Walter J. Hickel, 1966-1969
Keith Miller, 1969-1970
William A. Egan, 1970-1974
Jay Hammond, 1975-

Index

94

95

PICTURE CREDITS

ABOUT THE AUTHOR

With the publication of his first book for school use when he was twenty, **Allan Carpenter** began a career as an author that has spanned more than 135 books. After teaching in the public schools of Des Moines, Mr. Carpenter began his career as an educational publisher at the age of twenty-one when he founded the magazine *Teachers Digest.* In the field of educational periodicals, he was responsible for many innovations. During his many years in publishing, he has perfected a highly organized approach to handling large volumes of factual material: after extensive traveling and having collected all possible materials, he systematically reviews and organizes everything. From his apartment high in Chicago's John Hancock Building, Allan recalls, "My collection and assimilation of materials on the states and countries began before the publication of my first book." Allan is the founder of Carpenter Publishing House and of Infordata International, Inc., publishers of *Issues in Education* and *Index to U. S. Government Periodicals.* When he is not writing or traveling, his principal avocation is music. He has been the principal bassist of many symphonies, and he managed the country's leading non-professional symphony for twenty-five years.